Teenagers Ahead

David F. Slonaker

Nelson-Hall nh Chicago

Library of Congress Cataloging in Publication Data

Slonaker, David F
  Teenagers Ahead.

  Includes index.
  1. Children—Management.   2. Adolescent psychology.
3. Youth.   I. Title.
HQ772.S537   649'.1   79-16199
ISBN 0-88229-314-0 (cloth)
ISBN 0-88229-724-4 (paper)
Copyright © 1980 by David F. Slonaker

All rights reserved. No part of this book may be reproduced in any form without permission in writing from the publisher, except by a reviewer who wishes to quote brief passages in connection with a review written for broadcast or for inclusion in a magazine or newspaper. For information address Nelson-Hall Inc., Publishers, 111 North Canal Street, Chicago, Illinois 60606.

Manufactured in the United States of America

10   9   8   7   6   5   4   3   2   1

Contents

1	Learning: A Never-Ending Road	1
2	Communication: A Two-Way Street	15
3	Natural and Logical Consequences	27
4	Parents Are Models Too	35
5	Respect: A Give-and-Take Affair	47
6	Who Makes the Decisions?	57
7	Who Is Responsible?	69
8	Accentuate the Positive	83
9	What to Expect of Whom	91
10	Mapping a Vocational Route	103
11	Termination of Parenting—Continuation of Friendship	109
12	Conclusion	123
	Index	127

1
Learning:
A Never-Ending Road

Young children spend most of their time at home. Consider, for example, that by age ten, a child has completed 4 years of public school. Each school year consists of 180 days of 6 hours each. Multiply that by 4 years, and you have 4,320 school hours by age ten. Now consider how much time a child has spent at home by its tenth birthday: 24 hours a day times 365 days a year times 10 years equals 87,600 hours. This figure is reduced to about 54,080 waking hours at home. These 54,080 hours of parental influence amount to a time exposure that is over twelve times that of the school's 4,320 hours. Potentially, children can learn more at home than in any school. The responsibility thus falls on parents to make the home hours a valuable learning experience. In fact, children's life-styles are largely established before they encounter their first school experience. Certainly their personalities have jelled by their tenth birthdays.

These figures might be taken as an indication that it is time for parents to stop laying the blame for their children's shortcomings at the schoolhouse door. All the school's teachers and all the school's counselors cannot put a little child back together again when mommy and daddy are busily ripping the pieces apart. The odds are twelve to one against the school and its personnel. To blame society for the problems of the younger generation is only a further erosion of parents' responsibility for their children. For as long as children can count their years on their fingers, their parents *are* their society.

Parents can best prepare for their children's teen-age years—the worrisome ones—by concentrating all their child-rearing efforts on today and by using each of their 54,080 hours effectively. When parents turn their energies toward accomplishing today's parental tasks with excellence, they build a foundation unlikely to be shaken by teen-age unrest in the future.

Parents who for one reason or another cannot spend their allotted 54,080 hours with their children need to be especially aware of good child-rearing practices. Many educators and psychologists believe that a case can be made for offsetting part of the quantity component in the child-rearing formula with a quality component. In addition, a high-quality home environment need not be an expensive one. Quality environments occur when exploratory and learning-rich experiences are provided.

Controlling the Physical Environment

To obtain the desired quality, some parental control should be exercised over the environment. Parents frequently forget that direct control should be practiced over the environment, not over the children in the environment. The environment should be arranged so children can expect frequent but not necessarily certain success from their play and work. Young children should be free to manipulate their physical environment without the fear of damaging property that is part of an adult world. Certain sections of the house and yard can be made on-limits for children to explore without admonitions from parents.

When children have their own possessions and items that interest them in their environment, they are more inclined to care for and protect their possessions, because they have something to lose by not caring. Expensive vases, fine china, jewelry, and household cleaning chemicals have no place in the world of young children, but personal clothing, toys, pets, and books do have a place and can have considerable influence.

Controlling the Emotional Environment

Because of the long exposure children have to their parents, parents also have appreciable control over the emotional environment of their children as well as their physical environment. Providing a nurturing emotional environment involves no financial expenditures—only the expense of some parental psychic energy. One of the first adult environments into which children are socialized is the mealtime environment. Worth noting is the fact that children can only be truly socialized into the adult environment by adults who have themselves been socialized. A socialized adult is one who interacts effectively with other adults, one who is in touch with his or her own feelings and in touch with a great number of the feelings of others important in his or her environment.

One component of socialization includes the development of rational reactions to one's own mistakes, as well as to the mistakes of others. Children learn from their parents quite early how to respond emotionally to events in their environment. Unleashing a salvo of parental condemnation and cursing when little Randy overturns a half-full orange juice glass on the table rips the props from under a good relationship and constitutes no worthwhile learning. Useful learning, however, can be accomplished by informing the child that glasses can be placed on the table in more protected areas where there is less passing of dishes and movement of elbows.

A spill at the table can be used as a learning experience to teach children how to secure paper towels and wipe the table clean. The occasion can serve to let children know that the juice allotment for the meal has been used up and that no more is available until the next meal. All this can be done in a calm manner without anyone's jumping up from the table in a traumatic rage. No panic buttons need be pushed.

A mother told me of her six-year-old child who was just learning to ride a bicycle. As the parents sat on the patio with friends, they heard a crash. The mother peeked around the corner of the house to survey the damage. Little Judy did not see mother or anyone else at first as she looked up from the gouged turf where she and her new bike had taken a tumble. Momentarily, Judy stood up and was uprighting the bicycle when, out of the corner of her eye, she observed her mother's attentive look. Judy immediately fell to the ground, pulled the bike over on herself again, and began crying.

When a young child falls down and gets cut or bruised, it is too common for mother or father to come running to the rescue with a look of horror—or even with screams and shouts. But consider the effect of this. If a child has suffered a bad injury, a look of horror will not help, and screaming and shouting will only increase the chance of shock. If, however, no appreciable injury has taken place, it is perfectly reasonable for the parents to continue what they were doing before the incident without giving undue notice to the child. The child learns that it can be painful to fall down, but that one can usually get up and start over again after a fall. Children learn to fall a lot when they get undue attention from horrified parents with every accident. They also learn to cry a lot if crying has been effective in getting their parents' attention after each mishap, and children who are overattended with each bump, scrape, sniffle, or pain make the best candidates for adult hypochondriasis.

Here is another example of reinforcing undesirable behavior. Recently, friends visited the author's home and brought their five-year-old child who seemed calm enough and soon took a long afternoon nap. He awoke from his nap disgruntled and began to cry. The mother went into the room to console the child, but the whining and crying persisted. Finally the father became so irritated that he stormed into the room and said, "Give the kid anything he wants. Just so he stops that squalling." It is safe to say that there had been other similar scenes in the child's home. With two parents trying to gratify his wishes, these tantrum episodes must have become very rewarding. It was a sure way to get attention and occupy the parents' emotions.

If you, as a parent, like peace and quiet around the house, the best way to get tranquillity is to reinforce it when it occurs. Give children attention when they are quiet and pay them compliments on their behavior when it shows respect for other family members' rights. This is more effective, in the long run, than criticizing an uproar, which, even if it has any positive effect, will be short-lived.

Reinforcement works with parents as well. Parents learn to yell at children if the children's immediate response is to become quiet for a few minutes after each yelling episode. Attention from others who are significant to a child, whether they are parents, teachers, or peers, is so rewarding to many children that they will endure scorn and punishment in a classroom or at home to get it. And the worst punishment of all for these children is to receive no attention. When parents or teachers attend to children's inappropriate behavior and issue what they call punishment, it will likely be considered by the child a lesser punishment than complete inattention and, in fact, may be rewarding enough to encourage the child to repeat the behavior. Children, like adults, enjoy exercising power and control, and they are certainly achieving both when they occupy their parents' time, thinking, and emotions with undesirable behavior.

Learning by Association

A good principle to use in training children is learning by association. A boy learns to fish at a select spot along a creek with a particular bait at a certain depth because he associates this combination of conditions with earlier, pleasant experiences of catching fish. Any time a new lesson to be learned can be combined with something that a child already knows, a familiar base can serve as a mental peg on which to hang the new learning.

Learning by association can result in learning desirable lessons as well as learning lessons that result in unacceptable behavior. A child may learn to associate crying with getting attention. As long as the attention keeps coming, the crying will remain in the child's learned behavioral repertoire by the law of associative learning. Such an action may serve as an attention-getter for a child, but for an adult it will not automatically bring sympathetic, attention-giving adults to the scene. The child who has learned to associate crying with attention needs to unlearn this relationship if progress toward maturity is to be made.

Learning to fear wisely can also be a useful lesson for children in associative learning. Fear is an emotional state that prevents people from getting into situations they cannot handle—situations that may threaten their very existence. Fear of genuine threats in the environment is learned early and is functional in the self-preservation of the species. At times an overzealous mother and father may be extraordinarily careful in trying to insure that their children do not grow up fearful or inhibited. The result is frequently that their children reign as kings and queens at home; they have few frustrations as they travel an unrealistically smooth road paved with good intentions. They enter adulthood unprepared for the setbacks and frustrations they will inevitably encounter. It is, of course, undesirable to allow children to become so fearful of harmless events that phobias result, but this rarely is the case. If one visited almost any law enforcement agency in America, the officers would gladly discuss the fact that the world could use a few more inhibited individuals. Reasonable inhibitions, or if you prefer, the association of undesirable consequences with unlawful acts, represent desirable emotional learning. These emotions represent effective socialization of children into society in the form of reasonable inhibitions where the rights of others must be considered. Children need some inhibitions.

Households exist in which the word *no* is off limits. Modern parents are learning, however, that no as well as yes has an effective place in training children. A rational no from parents to children does not spell the shattering rejection that some therapists would have us believe. Permanent inhibitions or harmful associations are not developed when children are told no or otherwise restricted in a manner that proves to be reasonable and to their advantage.

Value Learning

Some schools of pyschology implore parents to avoid using words such as *yes, no, good, bad* and other so-called value words for fear of inadvertently imposing their values on their children. Yet why should parents denude themselves of useful learning tools, when all around them their children are exposed to evaluative feedback and the value systems of others. That ever-present electronic parent, the television set, constantly bombards children with evaluative commercials about the goodness of particular products. The national and international political news is full of evaluative overtones as viewers are exposed to the unbreachable chasm between cultures and subcultures. How many parents fool themselves into thinking they can react in a nonevaluative fashion and keep the lid on their value systems for twenty years of child rearing? And do they even want to downplay their values so totally in the face of other information sources that confront their children? They can rest assured that their children are doing two things: (1) reacting evaluatively to numerous environmental stimuli (Is this environmental occurrence good or bad for me? How does it affect and relate to me?) and (2) learning a system of values, whether it be from parents, television, or other, possibly undesirable, individual and organizational influences in their environment.

Humans are by nature evaluative, and a value system is a good thing to have. A value system gives one an anchored reference point against which to compare everyday occurrences.

Learning Complex Tasks as a Series of Simple Tasks

When children are learning a new task, it is important to avoid withholding favorable comment until perfection is achieved. Small positive steps in the correct direction are enough to expect at first, and they deserve favorable comment. The continuation of these positive steps will result in achievement of the completed task. Indeed it is a good idea to break large or complex tasks into small steps and present them one step at a time to children. Children must be able to see the light at the end of the tunnel when taking on new learning; they need to know that their actions are necessary, useful, and contribute to their goal. If a goal is too large or too distant, children cannot see that progress is being made, and they begin to think, "Oh, what's the use."

Learning to drive a car is an example of a complex learning task that can be taught in small steps with justified praise coming after each intermediate success. No child can be expected to calmly take command of an automobile in the initial stages of learning to drive it. Smooth starts, steady acceleration, gradual cornering, correct lane maintenance, and relaxed stops are all things that one acquires with practice. A driving lesson could begin with lesser goals in mind.

A teen-ager might begin by learning to identify the essential control devices on a car. A parent, in the role of teacher, could visually show how each device works and explain how it serves to control this or that function of the car. The child could then take advantage of psychomotor learning by sitting in the driver's seat with the ignition off and physically taking the car's controls through their range of movements. When the child first tries to operate a moving car, it should be made clear that neither parent nor child will expect perfection. The parent will need to avoid reacting with alarm or disgust at the poor control the child exercises over the car on the first trip. Concern over the possibility of an accident can be reduced to an acceptable level by driving in an open field or on a drivers' training track. In the same way a child should not be expected to learn to sew by starting to make a lined suit, but she or he could be expected to start sewing some of the seams on a plain skirt having no zippers. The same child should not be expected to learn to iron by starting on a ruffled, silk blouse, but could be expected to start by touching up a few wrinkle-resistant pillow cases after first watching someone who irons well. The ironer, as teacher, could explain why each particular movement is necessary and what would happen if the ironing were done in some other unsuitable manner.

A ten-year-old child cannot be expected to operate a riding lawn mower at high speed on a steep backyard dotted with trees and shrubs, but he or she can be expected to operate a push mower for a short time on a small area of level, dry, shrub-free lawn. The child will be better prepared initially if he or she has observed an adult and has been given a demonstration of the mower's basic functioning, along with the necessary safety precautions. Least of all, a child certainly does not need harsh criticism if he or she mows a wavering swath or leaves a patch of unmowed grass here and there. The attending parent has the responsibility of complimenting the child on the important parts of the job that are done correctly, such as keeping feet and hands clear of the rotating blade.

Training that Misses the Mark

Parents who are overly critical of their children at these early stages of learning are inadvertently teaching their children to expect too much of themselves. The parents' disappointment and unfulfilled expectations are transferred to their children when this happens. A feeling of not being good enough causes children to develop low self-esteem and to picture themselves as inadequate.

Some parents who ridicule and degrade their children's learning efforts do so from an unconscious motivation to prevent their children from surpassing them. They keep their children "in their place"—a place that seems to be subservient. The self-esteem of these parents is threatened by their children, yet the parents are not cognitively aware of the threat. One of the finer compliments that can be paid to parents is that they have excelled at child-rearing to the point where their children have surpassed them.

At the other extreme of this issue are the parents who do not feel threatened by their children's successes, but rather, are threatened by their children's failures. They overly identify with their children, feeling that their own personal fortunes ride on those of their children. More will be said about these parents in the chapter on expectations.

Have you ever overheard a parent say, "Oh! What am I going to do with little Bart? I just can't do anything with that child." Frequently the remark is said within hearing of the child. How does the message come through to a child? Something like this: "I am bad. I cause my parents' grief because of the bad things I do. They have no control over me. When I am bad, as I have just been, I win and they lose, because I get their attention and I control their behavior. See, they just admitted to another adult that I defeat them. I will continue to defeat them with this kind of behavior. They say I'm bad, so I must surely be bad. I might as well do what displeases them, because they think I am bad whether I am or not. I will live up to the picture they paint of me. I will fulfill the expectations they have of me."

All children want to be best at something, and Bart has just managed to be best at being the worst. He has lived up to what his parents have predicted for him. The mechanism of the self-fulfilling prophecy has caused his parents' expectations to be met.

Children can be trained without being bombarded with adverse criticism. Parents need to stop directing personal attacks at their children, attacks in which children are told how bad they are. Parents who generalize their criticism instead of calling attention to specific inappropriate activities give their children no idea why the activity was out of place and what it might better have been replaced with. Instead of leveling negative generalizations at children, it is better to inform children matter-of-factly of their specific, unacceptable behavior and tell why it is unacceptable.

"Because I say so" is never a sufficient reason to use in explaining "why" to a child. The "why" must represent the truth and be presented in terms the child can comprehend. When parents' reasoning is sound, a way can be found to explain their thinking at the appropriate age level of the child. If children brought to light the undesirable behavior that they see in their parents, there is little chance they could get away with saying, "Don't do that because I say so" Neither should their parents employ such weak reasoning. In pointing out specific, unacceptable child behavior, parents might mention to the child that, since most of his or her behavior is appropriate, the inappropriate behavior appears even more noticeable and out of place.

To maximize useful learning, children should think highly of their parents, just as parents should think highly of their children. If parents think highly of children, it shows in their actions toward the children. There is a difference between thinking highly of children and bragging about them. When parents brag and heap exaggerations on their children, they are really admitting that the children have not lived up to their high expectations, and thus, they find it necessary to stretch the truth about their children's accomplishments. Children's true accomplishments can speak for themselves.

In what ways do parents show that they do not think highly of their children? By saying such things as "Oh! That noise coming from the other room must be my kids. I just know it is. I can't do a thing with them. Why aren't they good like other kids?" Most parents have heard this and possibly have said it of their own children when they were with friends at church, in public, or at a club, and the children were disturbing others by running and making loud noises. In this type situation, when someone's children are being disruptive, it is time to remain quiet and play a listening role. Before long, another parent will likely start apologizing for his or her children. It seems socially acceptable and expected to criticize one's own children in front of other adults, even if the children are within earshot. In this case, however, the social norm is not healthy for the parent-child relationship.

If it is later learned whose children were creating the disturbance it is up to the parents of the disruptive children to talk with their children about the inappropriateness of the behavior. The reason the behavior was undesirable and the effect that it had on others can be explained.

One should be cautious not to accuse children unless one is certain they contributed to a commotion. When parents do not know the extent of their own children's involvement, they can still mention the disturbance to their children and state why it was inappropriate, but they should stop short of accusations, although the subject should not be dropped until parents have indicated a more appropriate behavior that could have been substituted. If the children proclaim their innocence, parents have no choice but to exemplify trust and accept their children's version of the story as they use the opportunity to tell the children what more acceptable behaviors could have been substituted by the offenders.

Parents can at some point expect to be given a compliment about their children. Justified compliments can be accepted graciously with no need at all to feel guilt due to excessive pride. It is certainly not necessary to say, "Oh, no. My children are just not that nice. That doesn't sound like my kids." Instead, it is totally appropriate to accept the compliment with a thank you. Then, above all else, pass it on to the children. They should be told the particular behavior that was complimented. Accentuating the positive builds children's self-images and is a vital part of development.

Favorable remarks to children must be sincere and not something tossed off for effect. Children know the difference. Fake flattery is obvious to children and causes them to feel they are not good enough to earn genuine compliments. Only justified praise takes root and nourishes healthy self-esteem.

Truth in compliments is also part of learning. For children and adults, learning is nothing more than becoming acquainted with truth. Truth is no more or less than the representation of facts. When people use truth to relate to children, they increase the probability that children will make good use of truth by calling upon it when they relate to others.

Parents need to learn to guide children without exercising overtraining. Comparing children with each other is a type of overtraining. The problem originates when parents try to train one child to be like another who is considered in some way to be a more desirable child. Perhaps one child is perceived to be better simply because he or she is less trouble to care for and causes the parents less distress. This child then becomes an example of the ideal child; other children are compared and found lacking. As humans, we are alike in many respects, but we are different in just as many other respects. And let us always work to preserve those differences. Our society needs a broad spectrum of individuals. As parents, let us stop trying to fit all our children into the same mold. Comparing the weaknesses of one child to the strengths of another serves to widen the separation and establish it permanently. Such comparisons get the unfavored child started in life with a poor self-image. The child grows up thinking that he or she is always being compared with others, that there is no way ever to be good enough. The child begins to think that it is his or her lot in life always to be inferior. This produces an adult who too frequently defers to others.

Consider the example of Johnny, who was just entering kindergarten as his older brother was finishing junior high school.

Johnny's father made a frequent point of reminding him that he did so little work around the house compared to that done by his older brother, Harry, when Harry was Johnny's age. He would say; "You don't do enough around this house to earn the salt that goes into your bread. Why, when Harry was your age, he used to cut firewood every day and start all the fires each morning before you even got out of bed." Although Johnny thought he did as much work to help run the household as other children his age, he began to accept his father's statements of his own inadequacy. Johnny entered adulthood with the negative "Why, when Harry was your age—"message still ringing in his ears. Johnny accepted the idea that his older brother really had done considerably more work around the house than he had done and he eventually learned to live with this "fact," which produced a feeling of guilt for his having been a lazy, inadequate shirker. The guilt feelings seemed less intense in Johnny's adult years, but in fact had only been repressed.

I thought this story was near a conclusion as Johnny sat across from me in my office. I had been just as surprised as Johnny when he found a long lost, yellowed diary in his parents' attic. Johnny said the real surprise came to him when he opened it to the time he was a high-school sophomore and read an entire year's worth of his most intimate secrets. What secrets had been locked within the yellowing pages for some twenty-five years? Did it tell of a passionate crush on his third-period English teacher? Did it note his unspoken plans to join the marines right after graduation?

What was to be revealed after a quarter-century of dust gathering? Nothing at all that even approached the glamour of the above subjects. The diary actually read more like a scientific log of household chores. Johnny could hardly believe the lackluster content of his diary. Who would ever write such unexciting entries as, "Planted potatoes in garden today. Cut more firewood. Firewood stack is now six feet high and fifteen feet long." Such entries were interspersed with equally unexciting accounts of autumnal activity that read, "Raked leaves today. Burned contents of trash cans on leaf pile. Waxed floors in house." Johnny read every page with astonishment, for every page was a chronicle of daily household chores. Johnny had trouble believing that this diary was his, the king of the shirkers.

Why did this person have to wait until he was in his forties to realize that he really did play an important role in the everyday activities of his childhood home? If his older brother had done more work than

Johnny had, then Harry must truly have been a whiz, but this should in no way detract from the fine efforts and many accomplishments achieved by Johnny in his teen-age years.

Condorcet offered great wisdom when he said, "Enjoy your own life without comparing it with that of another." This thought could easily be expanded to read: Give no one cause to comment that your children all came from the same mold. Children need not resemble each other or their parents in their behavioral patterns. Parents can expect their children to be different from each other by nature, and they should, by all means, promote this. Free from the pressures of comparison, children will gravitate toward their natural strengths.

Attitude Training

Parents have appreciable influence over their children's attitudes and moods. This parental influence is controlled in part by the modeling effect that is the subject of a later chapter. A word of caution is, however, in order at this point. Parental influence must not be like the control one exercises over a television set. People control a television set by selecting the station they want; they adjust the sound to their liking as well as the contrast, brightness, and hue. Children obviously are not television sets, and parents were never intended to control them on a direct basis. When a family's interactions approach the television analogy, the children reserve the right to exchange roles and tune out their parents psychologically as well as physically.

Training is not a process of controlling, but rather, a process of intelligent, well-directed influencing. Children should see in parents the very traits parents would like to see in their children. The traits and attitudes that parents would like to see in their children cannot be achieved by direct parental control. Rather, the process is an indirect one. Over a period of time, children will begin to reflect the attitudes and respect that adults have shown toward them and others.

Learning: A Lifelong Process

Learning occurs from the moment of birth. But when is learning finished? Never. The job of acquiring knowledge is a lifelong process that is never completed. One must seek to learn the lessons of truth all one's life. Each person has the responsibility of learning from all the persons with whom he or she has contact throughout the course of a lifetime.

Parents like to think that their children learn life's most valuable lessons from them. Parents, however, must also remain open to the possibility of learning equally valuable lessons from their children.

A parent recently told me of an insightful experience he had with his son. The father had referred his seventeen-year-old son to me for therapy, and I suggested that the father come for therapy as well, since most child problems are associated with interpersonal relations within the family. It was during one of our sessions that I became aware of the following incident.

> The son had traded cars twice recently and mentioned to his father that he was thinking of trading again. His father became alarmed and exclaimed, "What will people think? It won't look good to trade again so soon." The son countered with, "It won't look good to whom?" Click. The father experienced what psychologists sometimes call an Ah-ha reaction as he saw for himself a point I had been making in our sessions. Moreover, the son was a better teacher than I was, because the message from the son took just like a vaccination. The father had an important job and was often in the public eye, which made him feel "watched." He felt that, not only should his actions be acceptable to "his" public, but those of his family. The father had no right to impose his conceptions of the public's expectations on his son (or family), and he first internalized the insight of this fallacious view when his son asked, "It won't look good to whom?" Fortunately, the father was a willing learner even at the age of forty-four. He began to apply the lesson to his life immediately.

When I was a schoolboy, I could never seem to master standing my bicycle on its kickstand except on the firmest and levelest of ground. The same problem plagued me when I purchased a three-speed bike as an adult. I was startled one Sunday, to learn two great lessons from my eleven-year-old nephew. First, he commented matter-of-factly, "Uncle David, why don't you try turning your handlebars in the opposite direction when you use the kickstand?" Bells rang and lights flashed as I tried his practical suggestion and found it to be the answer to a twenty-five-year-old problem. How many times had I retrieved my over tipped bike from the mud? No more picking fallen bikes up off the lawn for me. I had learned to turn the handlebars away from the kickstand side to gain the required extra stability. Finally, I had learned this lesson belatedly at age thirty-three and I learned it from someone who was twenty years my junior.

The more important lesson, of course, was that every individual can learn something of value from every other individual. Adults need to continue learning from others and to instruct their children to be alert at all ages to learning opportunities that come from unlikely sources. Learning is a never-ending road.

2
Communication: A Two-Way Street

Why bother to tell children what understanding parents we are and that they can come to us with any of their problems and tell us everything? If this kind of desirable atmosphere for communication exists, parents need not tell their children; the children will know. On the other hand, if such an intimate exchange of thoughts does not exist, the children will be aware of this as well and will not trouble themselves to listen to what their parents are saying.

Starting Communication

How can we communicate to our children that they truly can share their innermost problems with us? We start when we stop. Yes, communication begins when parents stop, listen, and respond to their children as they come bounding in the door from school telling of some important event that happened during the day. And, of course, this may well happen when parents are busy, tired, or irritated. At such times some parents try to feign an interest in their children's activities. Yet, feigned attention to children at a time like this is not sufficient; in fact, it is never sufficient and will eventually turn off children just as surely as ignoring them will. Consider this situation: A father, on returning home from work, responds initially when his children approach him to tell of the day's happenings. As the children are unwinding, the father abruptly interrupts with some totally unrelated statement that he directs to the mother. He then turns to the children with a smiling facial gesture and a nod of the head, both of which are designed to indicate that he is still listening. Suddenly, another quick thought comes to his mind, which he immediately passes on to his wife.

How do the children feel? More important, how do they react? Children are more perceptive than most adults imagine, and they easily perceive where thoughts and attentions are truly directed. After a few frustrating episodes such as the one just described, a child begins to hesitate. Then the child stops trying. The decision to stop trying may be an overt action, but more likely, it will be an unconscious association between efforts to communicate with parents and a lack of reward in the form of being listened to. Either way, the result is the same. The child stops communicating.

Communication Turns Off Early

Parents might even learn to listen attentively to some things they already know when they are verbally bombarded by their children. If children are repeatedly silenced or ignored, they learn to avoid approaching their parents with their feelings and problems. Parents who repeatedly silence or ignore their young children should not be surprised to find that these children turn into teenagers who shut their parents out of their psychological lives, as demonstrated in this story of one of my clients named Susan.

> Mrs. F complained that her seventeen-year-old daughter completely ignored her. When asked for a recent example of such behavior, Mrs. F had an incident right at hand. It seems that Susan had come to the breakfast table that very morning with her usual long face. When her mother cheerfully asked, "Good morning, Susan, did you sleep well last night?," there was no response. Further questions by Mrs. F were equally unsuccessful in eliciting a response. How could any child be so ungrateful and unkind as not to speak to her own mother when the two were alone together? Investigation began to clarify this puzzling problem.
>
> It seems that when the children were small, Mrs. F had to take a job to supplement the family income. This meant that much of her time at home was spent busily cooking and sewing and cleaning. As one might expect, when Susan wanted to talk with her mother or show her mother something, the reception was not an overly welcomed one. In fact Susan's mother sat in my office and painfully related that, when the children interrupted at such times, she was frequently in a hurried, harried, anxious state and told them to shut up, go away, or not bother her.

Repeated episodes of this type over a period of years became a way of life for mother and daughter. This noncommunicative way of life, learned by Susan as a child, was extended into adolescence. Susan had learned that her verbalized observations and insights were not welcomed by her mother. The learned noncommunicative way of life cannot be altered overnight just because mother now has the time to listen—or should we say, now *takes* the time to listen.

Quite often, parents fail to get needed negative feedback from their children about their innocent but unsound child-rearing practices until their children are teen-agers. Then when things explode, parents wonder what has happened to cause their child to be so difficult, so aloof—so ungrateful. Parents today are inclined to look to the school or, more likely, to their teen-ager's peers for the cause. At best, they wonder what they, as parents, have done *recently* to trigger such an outburst. It is rare for parents to summon up enough courage and insight on their own to consider the possibility that the way in which they have interacted with their child for the last fifteen years could be having an effect on today's problem.

Freedom of Speech and Freedom from Speech

Americans swell with pride when they discuss their heritage, which includes freedom of speech. Yet there are still parents in homes in the land of the free who have never considered that this freedom could possibly refer to their own children.

Homes exist where the children are never free to speak, because the parents are continuously speaking to or for the children. In such homes there is a *speaker* and a *speakee*. I prefer to think of the children of these homes as speakees instead of by the usual term, *listeners*. They actually learn, after some time, not to listen, and they give few, if any, replies to their parents. There is no communication in such a home, only talking. Children in speaker/speakee homes need protection of their "freedom from speech." They need to be free of the constant verbal bombardment from their parents.

Another type of speaker/speakee home involves an attenuation of speech by all parties rather than the parental verbal bombardment. In the speech-attenuated home the children's frequency of speaking has been reduced to nearly zero in a parental effort to suppress the feelings of the children. Haim Ginott has correctly stated in his book, *Between Parent and Child*, that "strong feelings do not vanish by being banished." A client told me of her father, who banished feelings on a regular basis. It was not uncommon for the father to hold an untenable position when she, her brothers, or even her mother were in disagreement with him. Not only did he refuse to listen, he refused to let other family members exercise their freedom of speech. At such times my client said she would try to make reasonable, logical counterpoints, but was met by a "dryp" from her hostile, red-faced father. He would allow no one in the family to disagree with him. She stated that the word *dryp* was actually a contraction of the words *dry up*, which was the father's way of demanding that the speaker be quiet and voice no further disagreement with him. He had spoken the final word and that was that.

Such a father should not expect his children or spouse to ever share a problem with him that might lead to his disapproval. The kinds of communications that eventually develop in a family of this type appear to be misleadingly cordial. An outward appearance of cordiality in a family can be dictated, but when it is not genuine harmony, the cost is great. For every dictator, there must be at least one dictatee. Eventually, each dictatee learns the rules of the game and is subdued into compliance. The dictatees may outwardly appear to be congenial, calm, and satisfied persons. They may succeed in repressing from their conscious thoughts their anger at what is happening to them. But at an unconscious level, there is the awareness that they are the losers in an unjust power struggle.

Dr. Smiley Blanton commented in his book, *Child Guidance:* "The age old adage that 'children should be seen and not heard' was devised, it may be sure, not by a child, but by some adult who wished to do the talking."

Children should be seen and heard. Children can learn to listen and learn to be listened to. Their conversational rights are much like those of any adult. Children deserve to be listened to when they do not interrupt others while talking and do not dominate the conversation. This type of conversational respect should be expected from adults as well.

Communicating is a two-way street. Any attempts at one-way communication from parents to children will be met with about as much enthusiasm as driving in the left lane of a two-way street. One-way communication is not only unpopular, it is quite dangerous to children's emotional health as well.

Listening to Children
A Place to Start

Henry Ford said, "If there is any one secret of success, it lies in the ability to get the other person's point of view and see things from his angle as well as from our own." Those who wish to be successful parents should certainly consider Ford's advice. Any time a parent can avoid being caught up in his or her own views to the point of excluding the child's views, there is opportunity for this success principle to function. And one of the best ways to get the other person's view is to remain quiet and listen to that person.

When parents complain that their children do not listen to them, it is safe to assume that the opposite situation exists as well. Parents whose children avoid listening to them can start the communication process in the correct direction by increasing the listening that they do. A part of good listening is the active consideration of some of the ideas and suggestions that others introduce. Children's self-images are nourished when parents use suggestions and alternatives introduced by the children. Whenever a child's ideas are as good or nearly as good as the parent's original plans, the child's approach should be followed. This teaches children to place value on their own thinking because they see their parent's valuing their suggestions. If a child's suggestion cannot be adopted, the child should be told why. Even if an idea cannot be put into practice, it can be held in a favorable light and not discredited. The idea can be kept in reserve for use at a time when it would be more applicable. Parents would do well to solicit actively ideas and suggestions from their children and to adopt their perspectives whenever possible.

Do you know of parents who actively solicit advice from their children? Children add to their feelings of self-worth when they are asked questions they can answer correctly, and they relish the opportunity to state their advice. Moreover, children are more inclined to accept decisions, plans, and actions that they have helped to formulate.

Advice sought from children does not have to concern earth-shaking philosophical matters of long-range, life-or-death importance. It can be as simple as asking a 13-year-old child whether she thinks it is best to mow the lawn on Saturday or to wait until the first of the week. If a son or daughter mows the lawn at 13, and I think they are capable and should, this will give the child a good chance to develop his or her decision-making ability. Allowing a son or daughter to choose the mowing day provides an opportunity to have some control over the immediate environment. So what if he or she decides to wait until Monday and the lawn is a little ragged on Saturday. It will keep. Since this was the child's decision, he or she will be inclined to do a better job on Monday than would have been done on Saturday.

If friends are coming for dinner in the near future, it is reasonable to expect a teen-ager to help in preparing the meal. But if the teen-ager is going to share in the work and responsibility, he or she should also share in the planning. Since the mother may have knowledge about the constraints of the budget, as well as information about the tastes of the guests, this would seem to indicate that the teen-ager does not have sufficient information to exercise total decision-making power. Being aware of this, the mother could narrow the menu alternatives and approach her teen-ager something like this: "I've been trying to think what we could serve when the Lawrences come over tomorrow. We simply can't afford to have steaks on the grill or that shrimp creole that we like so well. Still, I do have some other ideas about what the Lawrences will enjoy. Looks like it may be between the tuna casserole, grilled hamburgers, or maybe fried chicken. What do you think?" The power to say what will be served to the guests is now placed in the teen-ager's hands. The teen-ager can choose between the three alternatives, or, with a receptive mother, can introduce a fourth possibility. In any event the teen-ager will certainly be more interested in and derive greater satisfaction from preparing the meal since he or she has had the final say in what is to be served.

Problem Sharing without Assigning Blame

The first consideration in preparing to discuss a touchy subject is to question whether or not the subject really needs to be brought up. Before mentioning a subject, it should be confirmed that something can be gained by introducing the topic. Mere ventilation of parental feelings without constructive intentions to solve the problem plays no useful role in today's parenting.

After confirming that a contentious subject does merit further mention, the general tone should be nonaccusatory. Even when parents feel that the child has erred, there is simply nothing to be gained through hostility and adverse criticism that only serve to put a child on the defensive. This defensiveness is exemplified by a sudden refusal to communicate, a refusal to consider any parental suggestion, or a complete submission, which leaves the child with feelings of helplessness and powerlessness. When parents are open and receptive to ideas that are not in keeping with their own thinking, their children also are more likely to maintain a receptive frame of mind. This allows parents to introduce novel ideas to the children in a less traumatic manner.

The assumption that arguments favoring a child's view will be harmful if recognized or responded to by parents is an unhealthy one. It is also unhealthy thinking to assume that these problems will go away if not addressed. Points favoring the child's view can be recognized and dealt with, rather than being ignored in order to push ahead with a one-sided parental presentation.

Mr. A had thought it ridiculous when his thirteen-year-old daughter, Tammy, wanted a trail bike. His princess was no tomboy. Besides, what would the neighbors think? So when Tammy introduced the subject, he countered with these and other equally obvious (to him, anyway) objections and said there would be no more of this talk.

Tammy was prepared to introduce evidence supporting her reasoning:

1. Girls do things today that used to be considered strictly boys' business twenty years ago.
2. It is not necessary to have a license for off-the-road use of a trail bike.
3. Tammy had a good safety record with her bicycle.
4. Trail bikes can be equipped with mufflers so they don't become a noisy nuisance in the neighborhood.
5. Tammy knew of a good, used trail bike for only $175.

Indeed, she did know of a good used bike for $175, because this is just how much she had been able to produce by saving several years of birthday and Christmas money and adding it to her savings from her allowance, babysitting, and pop bottle return funds. On her own she made an outright cash purchase from an older child who owned the used bike and proudly rode into her parents' carport to display this, her first major purchase with her own money.

Tammy had not expected her parents would be so upset with the purchase. Why should they be? She had heard for the last two years how her own money was hers to do with as she saw fit. When she reminded her parents of this, they at first continued unabated in their raving. Later they became calmer as they considered the truth and rationality of her statements and her action, based on what she had been told about her ownership rights and decisions.

Mr. A had assumed that Tammy's desire for a trail bike would vanish if her repeated requests and reasonings were ignored. He learned of this fallacy in his thinking the hard way, but at least he had the good judgement not to turn her independent action into a major catastrophe. He and his wife did learn to elicit, listen to, and consider their daughter's thinking more frequently. They also learned that Tammy was a shrewd trader who had made a wise purchase in a responsible manner. Communication would never go unattended at the A residence again.

Techniques of Introducing Discussion Topics

There are times when parents want to get a particular message across to their children. Messages to children, and to adults as well, come across better when they are tied in with what has just been said in the conversation. The message is more readily accepted when the parent can go along with the child's train of thought for a while before introducing the message. Interjecting a new thought without first tying it into the preceding conversation is like jumping on a moving parade float without first running alongside to attain the same speed as the float. Dropping message bombs into the conversation out of the blue can be avoided. The avoidance of message bombs will in turn encourage children to avoid dropping message bombs of their own into parental conversations.

Sometimes parents will find it necessary to be the bearers of unwelcome tidings. It is possible to take some of the sting out of certain important but unwelcome messages by first noting a child's mood and allowing this to determine when the message is introduced. There are times when an important message can be delayed for a few hours without disastrous consequences.

Messages that are likely to trigger disagreement can be softened by introducing the sensitive part after the areas of agreement have been brought to light. It is worth the effort to try to establish a receptive atmosphere before a likely point of disagreement is introduced.

Sometimes fathers and mothers block out incoming messages by being too concerned about what they want to say next. In such cases parents could create a rapport more quickly by not operating from a prepared text. A parental text need not be written on a piece of paper, it simply means that a parent has everything laid out in his or her mind that needs to be said—that is, everything that needs to be said *according to the parent*. Such preplanned attacks tend to block any incoming messages from the child. An agreement, or at least an understanding, of the separate positions could be facilitated more readily by actually listening to the child and then responding, based on what the child has said. The child's strong points will be acknowledged by understanding parents, instead of being degraded and counterattacked.

Much of the time children will do what their parents request, if the parents will first stop and take the time to listen to their children's views. While listening to the children's points of view, parents need to be open to the possibility that their children may have a better approach. Every family member should be willing to listen to every other family member with the idea that one's mind might be changed.

This rarely practiced phenomenon is called *respecting other's beliefs*. We hear it preached frequently, along with the current concerns for an individual's civil rights. We say we believe in respecting others' beliefs, yet we often fail to practice this worthwhile activity in our own homes where the need is greatest.

We find it too easy to blast children with a sure-fire comeback when a disagreement is in progress. At first it is difficult for parents to puzzle over a problem and hold a tight reign on verbal blasts that seem at the time to summarize the situation so perfectly; however, it is certainly more useful to adopt this open, problem-solving approach that avoids charging headlong into premature closure of problems.

Communicating Sex Information

Often parents with preteen children want to know how to handle delicate subject matter such as the discussion of sex. Such subject matter is generally more difficult for parents to discuss than it is for today's generation of children to assimilate. What if the child asks about sex? As parents, most of us know the answers to the majority of the child's questions relating to sex. Therefore, these questions can and should be answered as accurately as possible. A full-scale oratory should be avoided, as should unnecessary details that were not part of the question. Let us bury the stork story with the generation that started it. There is no need to take the child into his or her room and formally announce, "Now, it is time we had a talk about the birds and the bees." A child's questions come at unexpected times and places. Occasionally one question may lead to another and to another as parents' faces get redder and redder.

This happened at our dinner table. Our nine-year-old daughter felt she should show embarrassment at her ten-year-old brother's questions about sex and my willingly given answers. She ran from the room, but stuck her head through the door with her hands over her ears and an unforgettable, quizzical, grimacing look on her face. She wanted to hear the answers, but she had learned that, in our culture, she should not show such an interest about sex in front of adults. My son kept the questions coming—each of which was greeted with a matter-of-fact answer that included some of the more common slang words that children hear and whisper at school. Suddenly, my son said, "Thank you, Father, for today's sex lesson. Tune in tomorrow, folks, to your friendly station for the remainder of our story." At that, he and his sister went to his room, locked the door, and with much sniggering and whispering reviewed the session while their mother and I stared at each other in disbelief. No longer did my wife have to wonder how she would sit down and introduce her daughter to the subject of menstruation. No longer need my agenda on child-rearing contain a note to introduce a formal birds-and-bees, heart-to-heart talk.

Finding Time to Communicate

Many parents claim that they can never find time for their children. A parent may never *find* time. As we approach the twenty-first century, if you think that good parenthood is as important as I do, you will *make* time for your children. Time given begrudgingly to children does not count, children are quick to pick up a parent's wish to be somewhere else. Mothers and fathers occasionally need to plan ahead to take the time to set adult concerns aside for a while and relax with their children.

If the particular time in question is absolutely unavailable, it is better to tell the child that certain other things must necessarily be completed first. This presents an opportunity for the parents to let the child know that they will not always be busy with adult concerns, and that they do want to get together later. Another time could be established when the parents expect to be free for parent-child time sharing. It is not necessary to set a prearranged time and promise a son or daughter that you will be available then. Certainly, such a promise should not be made if the parents have any doubt about their ability to keep the promise to be available at the designated time. Continually putting off a child must not become a way of life in the family. On the other hand when delays in time sharing are rare, they are usually accepted as legitimate by the child.

Some parents feel they must constantly be talking with their children, either issuing instructions or asking questions. They think they are bridging the generation gap when they talk continuously. These parents should consider their own anatomy, noting that they have two ears and only one mouth. They would do well to use these communication modes in this same ratio and do two parts of listening for every one part of talking. Nothing, absolutely nothing, does more to remove a communication gap than giving two parts of genuine listening to every one part of talking.

Questions Can Be Harmful

Have you ever noticed how questions can be used to turn off someone? Conversations can be controlled and directed to a great extent by the nature of the questions asked. When questions are filled with implications and accusations, one can expect children to withdraw from the conversation at some point. Rather, it is much more invigorating to sprinkle conversations with questions children will enjoy answering—questions whose answers will show the children in a favorable light and give them an opportunity to show how much they know.

In an earlier section we discussed how questions are useful in seeking the advice and suggestions of children. Now we learn that questions can be conversation stoppers when used improperly. Mr. and Mrs. Q approached me wondering why their use of questions was not having the desired results on their domestic scene. I asked them to use a long-play tape recorder to record several days of family conversation on tape. I later collected and edited the tape. I had only to sample two hours of family conversations drawn from four twelve-hour days of family interaction to see the problem. Sure enough, the questions were there—all seventy-seven of them. The communication-stopping questions were along these lines:

- Joey, shouldn't you get up now so mother doesn't have to call you any more for breakfast?
- Nancy, why do you always squeeze the middle of the toothpaste tube?
- You're not taking that same girl to the dance tonight, are you, Charles?
- Oh, don't you like your good, hot oatmeal?
- Nancy, have you misplaced your books again?
- Joey, you don't really want to take Early Civilization next year when you could still get into the geometry class, do you?
- Did you really pay $18 for *that* dress?
- Do you think I'm made of money?
- How many times do I have to tell you to hang up your coat?
- What kind of grade do you think you'll get with that paper?

Whenever parental questions show disgust or disregard for children's feelings, they are received by children as items that deserve no serious consideration.

Joke with Children— Not about them

A few parents make a habit of teasing their pre-teen and teen-age children. A child's sense of humor is often not fully developed at these ages. In addition, what parents imply in jest is sometimes what they really think at a lower level of consciousness. They know that such a thought would not be acceptable presented in an outright manner.

When parents can joke about themselves and become the brunt of their own jokes, there are no particular problems. But when a child is continually the brunt of a parent's jokes, the child takes it as a putdown. And it may well have been intended as a putdown by an unsuspecting parent. Children learn to dislike parents who are always kidding at the expense of the children. Some parents even use their frequent jesting and teasing to raise their own self-images at the expense of their child's self-image.

Surprises Aren't Always Child-Pleasers

Parents can expect children to spring fewer surprises on them when they as parents do an adequate job of keeping their children informed. Children are especially resistant to last-minute announcements that guests are coming for dinner, or that the family is going somewhere in a few minutes. Children like to be aware of family vacation plans and trips well in advance. The best way to make them aware is to get them involved with the planning. Children do not care about all the latest news and current events, but they do like to know about plans that involve them.

Children Can Fire Parents

Parents can be fired physically or psychologically. Parents are fired physically when a child runs away from home. Parents are fired psychologically when a child reluctantly decides to stay at home but terminates all communication of feelings with the parents. When psychological firing occurs, the child will voice only those comments that are absolutely essential for him to function within the family. The case of Susan and her mother, Mrs. F, is an excellent example of a mother who was fired psychologically.

A Time to Listen—
A Time to Ignore

There is a time to listen and a time not to listen. Parents should stop listening when children use the weapons of crying, anger, withholding love, or temper tantrums as means of intimidating others to give in to them or not to disagree with them. Children may threaten a temper tantrum or another contrived, objectionable personality display to force their parents into giving in to their demands. Additional notice in the form of listening, pleading, and other attention-giving responses by parents should be avoided on these occasions. Children can be trained to know that responsible behavior is expected from them even when they do not get their way. Children learn to abandon irrational, irresponsible behavior to further their selfish motives when their parents refuse to reward such selfish behavior.

3
Natural and Logical Consequences

Natural consequences can best be described as what happens when a child, or anyone, for that matter, touches a hot stove. Most persons learn fairly early in life not to touch exceedingly hot objects. Nature is a good and thorough teacher—although a bit harsh at times. Allowing nature to take its course—called natural consequences—involves no action or decision making on the part of either parent. In natural consequences the cause-and-effect relationship takes over.

When the father of six-year-old Paulette took her and her brother to an ice cream parlor, she was delighted. The cone of butter almond ice cream was indescribably delicious, although she found it necessary to try to describe it to her brother as she waved it carelessly in front of him. The natural laws of gravity prevailed as she swung the cone and tilted it a bit too far. Splop! Who could say anything? The lesson was there if her father and other nearby adults would allow it to be learned. Her father's first impulse was to run back to the ice cream parlor for another butter almond ice-cream cone for Paulette.

Two passers-by insisted on replacing her cone. Father called them off by saying he would take care of it, and take care of it he did. He did not fuss, scold, or threaten. He was sorry it happened and offered his regrets as he stated that it would probably be another week before they would be back by the ice cream store. He suggested that her next cone would enjoy a better fate if she would hold it upright with a minimum of swinging motions.

At this point, Paulette's brother, Ronney, offered her three-and-a-half licks from his cone of strawberry. His offer was readily accepted. Strawberry had never before tasted this good to Paulette. This unexpected aside gave Ronney the opportunity to feel good about his altruistic behavior in sharing his cone with Paulette, and it was a model of generous behavior for Paulette. Ronney decreased the chances for future selfishness and exclusive ownership behavior between himself and his sister. Father recovered from his guilt feelings for not rushing back to the ice cream parlor for a replacement when he saw his son's altruism and the lesson his daughter could learn from the incident.

Natural Consequences—A Learning Opportunity

Any time a parent can allow the natural consequences of a child's behavior to have their effect, a more lasting change toward desirable behavior will be accomplished. Parents automatically give positive reinforcement to desirable behavior and negative reinforcement to undesirable behavior when they manage to stay out of the picture enough to permit natural consequences to play their role.

Letting nature direct the course of events is a more useful technique than a situation where a parent arbitrarily sets the standards for good and bad and—issues punishment. With natural consequences the child is able in most instances to understand what has happened and why. Parents may want to help with the why by explaining sequentially how behavior A leads to result B. This is best done in a step-by-step nonpunitive manner. A child can then identify any undesirable results with the behavior that just occurred. When the natural consequences of a child's behavior are allowed to happen, the child is inclined to better understand a cause-and-effect relationship and less likely to perceive an effect as some arbitrary punishment imposed by a vindictive parent.

The Limits of Natural Consequences

There are occasions when it is necessary to interfere with natural consequences in order to protect adequate health, safety, or property rights. Persons who interact with children will see fit to attenuate the effects gained from natural consequences in certain cases, an example of which might be the need to interfere with the consequences of a child's running in front of a moving car. To be struck with a car is allowing natural consequences to go too far.

More often than not, parents tend to intervene too much rather than too infrequently. Parents have a natural propensity to come to their child's rescue, to set the record straight, to make their thinking known, and to exercise their judgements. Actions of this type can get in the way of natural consequences that would otherwise have resulted from the child's actions. Before parents interfere with or prevent natural consequences from happening, they should be sure that the consequences present a significant threat to the health and safety of their child or other affected persons. It is better to allow a child to be inconvenienced or uncomfortable than to interrupt a valuable, natural learning experience. Such learning opportunities, when experienced by children, are often carried into adulthood as valuable assets. But more succinctly, if no person's health or safety is seriously threatened, and a parent cannot decide whether to get involved or not, it is better to do nothing.

If only Mrs. L could have done nothing when her son, Rod, failed to get up early enough to catch the special bus for the school field trip to the state fair. She was angry and blamed her son, but she also felt a bit guilty at the thought of not bailing her son out. She felt obligated to come to the rescue as she slung her raincoat over her pajamas, jumped into the car with a pleading Rod, and tore out of the driveway into the morning's fog. She gave Rod a tongue lashing as she chased after the bus, which had a fifteen block lead. Caution lights were treated as green lights; red lights were treated as caution lights, and stop signs became caution signs as Mrs. L and Rod carved a wreckless trail through the rush-hour traffic. Thirty minutes later, she placed her son on the bus with a final admonition and threat.

What would have happened if Mrs. L had done nothing—had just simply allowed Rod to miss the trip to the state fair? Mrs. L could have gotten dressed for work in her usual unhurried manner. Rod could have been allowed to plead for his mother to rescue him as she reminded him that he would need to remember to get up earlier and watch his time more carefully the next time a special bus was used for a class field trip. Mrs. L could have reminded Rod that, since he had missed the special bus, he would be expected to catch the regular school bus and attend classes as usual. Mrs. L could have refused to be intimidated. She could have avoided Rod's efforts to try to make her feel guilty—to make her feel as if she were a "bad mother." She could have remained uninvolved as her son acquired a valuable learning experience.

Augmenting Natural Consequences: Letting Children Correct Their Mistakes

It may sometimes be desirable to augment and amplify natural consequences to strengthen their reenforcement power and to make learning more complete and applicable to life. For instance, when a child comes in with his or her best shoes muddy after having been told that these shoes should not be worn in the mud, the natural consequences of this situation are that the child will have to live with the muddy shoes and wear them on dress occasions. A less natural but perfectly logical consequence could be to allow the child to clean the shoes. It is the parents' responsibility to teach the child how to complete the task, but it is not the parents' responsibility to clean the shoes for the child. The child is responsible for returning the shoes to their original state. When the child reports that the shoes are clean, one parent should confirm this by checking the shoes without coming to any foregone conclusions. The care of any inspection will need to be adjusted according to the child's age and experience with this type of activity. For example, if the shoes are not cleaned to their original state, and the child is capable of achieving this, the parent should carefully withhold statements such as, "That is all wrong . . . you are no good . . . I'd rather do it myself."

Perhaps the parents would rather complete the task themselves, but this temptation must be avoided. It would be easier in many cases for the parent to take over and complete the task for the child. It could even be completed in less time by the parents, but this would take away from the child a much-needed opportunity to learn self-discipline.

A more useful learning experience can be accomplished for the child in this case if the parents acknowledge the shoe cleaning progress in an objective and friendly manner. The parent can then go further, if necessary, and point out what is still lacking to achieve satisfactory completion of the job. Suggestions or a brief demonstration can be given to show how the job can be adequately completed. This tells the child that it is possible to achieve what is being requested.

When the job is satisfactorily completed (satisfactory is best determined by the child's age and experience with such tasks) acknowledgment of the completed task is in order. Most likely, the child has learned two lessons when logical consequences have prevailed: (1) to wear good dress shoes outside only in nonmuddy areas, and (2) how to clean muddy shoes.

Advantage can be taken of the opportunity to show the child what shoes would be more appropriate to wear when playing in the mud. This method does appear to take more time and effort than is required if the parent goes ahead and cleans the shoes and "lets the child off the hook," but the real time savings results in the future, when the parents are saved the task of slaving over their child's muddy shoes. Parents should not suffer because of their children's inappropriate behavior, but rather, should supplement the learning process and point the child in the direction of acceptable behavior. "Acceptable behavior" may be interpreted rather narrowly by some parents. This is satisfactory so long as it does not confine the child's life space so it permanently impedes intuitive learning tendencies. Other parents may interpret "acceptable behavior" with less rigidity—even to the point of allowing their children to do or say some things that they would rather be left undone and unsaid. Their thinking might be that they wish to see their children blazing their own trails as opposed to carefully following in their parents' footsteps.

When individual parents have worked through their interpretation of acceptable behavior, they can help their children understand this interpretation by a modification of natural consequences that is often referred to as logical consequences.

Logical Consequences

Whereas natural consequences result without any involvement from persons in a child's environment, logical consequences result when there is some parental action to achieve behavior modification on the part of the child involved in a specific situation. Logical consequences are best demonstrated when parental intervention is minimal and is arranged to lead to a consequence that the child concludes is genuinely a rational, reasonable result of his or her behavior.

One father instigated an unnatural, illogical consequence by insisting that his children give away their tropical fish when the children became confused over whose day it was to feed the guinea pig and clean the cage. Getting rid of the fish was hardly a natural or logical consequence of failing to care for a guinea pig. A natural consequence would have been to let the pig go unattended and take a chance on the guinea pig's starving or dying of thirst before the odor from the uncleaned cage caught the children's attention. For a parent who doesn't believe in cruelty to animals, a better logical consequence would be to give the guinea pig to another caring family or to place a moratorium on new pets in the household. It would certainly have been accepted as a more logical result of the children's failure to carry through on their responsibility.

Planning On-Time, Accident-Free Meals

Some action or decision-making is generally involved by parents when they allow their children to experience the logical consequences of their actions. Logical consequences involve situations such as allowing children to go without dinner when they come in from play at 6:30 p.m. in a home in which dinner is served at 6:00 p.m. It seems logical that, if children are not there when the food is on the table at the announced time, those children have just missed a meal. Most children will have little trouble accepting this consequence. Although they may voice complaints and claim they have been dealt with unfairly the first few times, they will soon learn to be on time for meals.

If a child becomes careless at the dinner table and overturns his or her milk, it is reasonable and logical to expect the child to clean up the table and floor immediately. No replacement of the milk or other drink would be a further logical consequence of this behavior. There is no need to accuse the child or to consider whether or not the action was deliberate or accidental. The result of a table spill is the same whether or not the action is an accident. Thus, it is appropriate to let the consequences be the same in either event. It is truly surprising how fast children can learn to handle glasses of liquid without upsetting them after they have been asked to be responsible for their behavior a few times. Practicing logical consequences at the table has a way of reducing the accident rate quickly. Children's psychomotor activities are not fully developed and coordinated at an early age, and this may lead to accidents in handling food and other objects. Nevertheless, parents need not repeatedly experience the consequences of their child's accidents.

Some children enjoy seeing their mothers fume as they clean up their children's mess or collect knocked-over vegetable cans at the supermarket. When these so-called accidents happen, a mother would do well to hold on to her temper and simply instruct the child to put things back the way they were, as nearly as is possible. The child should be allowed to share the natural embarrassment along with his or her mother when an "accident" takes place in a public setting. On the other hand, there is nothing to be gained by calling so much attention to the instance that a child feels unfairly treated. Neither mothers nor fathers need be slaves to their children's untidiness. The natural consequence of allowing the perpetrator of accidents to pick up the pieces will help insure that a child does not become addicted to his or her own untidiness for long.

By allowing children the opportunity to be responsible for their actions, parents do their children a great favor. Here is an example from my childhood, which was spent on a hilly farm in eastern Tennessee. At age twelve, my father and older brothers were in the process of teaching me to drive the family car—a 1939 Chevrolet. After completing the morning's work in the fields, we headed homeward in the Chevy with me at the wheel. The pasture was rutted and bumpy from cow paths. I cautiously approached a gap in the fence with the car in low gear. Misjudging the opening, I crashed into a solid locust corner post at fifteen miles per hour. The post proved to be quite sturdy. Floundering for the brake pedal in the confusion, I accidentally hit the accelerator pedal and floored it. The old Chevy kept running, spinning its wheels into the turf for a couple more reverberations off that sturdy locust post. The front left fender was a shambles. I said fearfully, "Let me out of this thing." Guilt and fear were running high in my childish mind, but my father was surprisingly calm. He said, "Son, keep your seat. You got us into this, now you get us out." I restarted the motor, backed off, took careful aim, drove safely through the gap, and completed the drive home for lunch. The fender was repaired more quickly than my pride was.

What learning took place from my driving experience? I learned that constant visual feedback is necessary when driving an automobile, and that adjustment and compensation must be made as account is taken of the visual feedback. I learned that failure to respond to visual feedback can result in automobile accidents. I learned that mistakes can be made and the objective still reached. I learned to take responsibility for my actions. I learned to complete tasks that were started. I learned that I could drive a car just as well after the accident as before. In fact, I could drive better, because to this day, I have never hit another fence post. And I certainly learned about the toughness and durability of those locust fence posts we had so carefully placed in service on the farm.

Too Much Success—An Unnatural Consequence

The natural consequences of human activity are such that goals are sometimes reached. These same natural consequences at other times lead to goals that are frustrated and left unattained. Excessive interference (disruption of natural consequences) on the part of parents who always try to set up winning situations for their children can result in children who grow up expecting always to win—always to be successful. Children whose successes have mostly been artificial frequently feel that society owes it to them always to allow them to win. A child who is always successful becomes a selfish adult with self-gratification at the top of his or her need list. And, of course, as children grow older, their parents will not always be there to set up success situations, and their winning streak will eventually be broken.

When this strange (to them) phenomenon happens in their adult years, it is particularly difficult for these hard losers to adjust to temporary failure. They may become discouraged and depressed and eventually quit trying. A sprinkling of early temporary failures is the spice needed to add flavor to the also necessary early successes.

A child, or an adult as well, who never loses is either getting outside help with life's outcomes or is playing his or her cards too close to the chest. Such a person is overly fearful of failure and is not venturing far enough to risk the chance of failure. To always play life so safe as to never lose is to tamper with one's own potential greatness and to stifle one's chances for self-actualization. Thus, it is possible for a child to experience too much success, if this success results from someone's sacrifice and hard work rather than from the child's efforts.

4
Parents Are Models Too

All models do not appear on magazine covers. Models also appear in homes all across the land. The models found in homes are called *parents*. A model is something or someone that is established as an example or a pattern to be followed. Children model much of their behavior on the behavior they see in their parents. The way parents deal with disappointment and failure becomes incorporated into the behavioral patterns of children, just as parents' methods of dealing with success become part of their children's thinking and acting. "What you are speaks so loud that I cannot hear what you say," is an expression that most adults have heard; however, some parents act as if they had never heard this statement when they tell their children one thing and then do another themselves.

Mothers and fathers could profitably spend time watching their young children involved in a role-playing game. If the children are playing house, mother and father can watch how closely a little girl emulates her mother in word and in actions. Fathers can get a true picture of what their sons are learning from them by watching their sons' play-acting. Sometimes the picture of ourselves that we see portrayed by our children is not an expected one—and sometimes it is not even a desired one.

Objective observation gives parents valuable feedback. They can take advantage of the feedback by putting it into use as they modify their own behavior to bring it more into line with that which they wish to exemplify to their children.

Communication modeling is one of the first things most children learn. A child is less likely to make a habit of interrupting parents while they are talking if the parents respect the child's thoughts by not interrupting the child when the child is engaged in conversation. This is one more example of the opportunity parents have to exemplify the behavior that they expect from their children. A child who continues to interrupt can be asked to take his or her turn speaking as soon as the parent finishes speaking. When the children are interrupted by their parents, nondefensive parents who can be objective to feedback from their children can expect to be reminded by the children of the need not to interrupt an ongoing statement.

Conversations among parents and children should flow naturally without the necessity of anyone's feeling overly sidetracked for an extended period of time while waiting for a chance to enter the conversation. Parents can best show desired conversational behavior by freely listening to and directing statements to each other and to their children without requiring the children to deal with the leftovers of a topic after the parents have talked it to death.

Showing Gratitude

Gratitude is not one of the more common attributes of human nature. Humans set themselves up for disappointments by expecting gratitude after doing favors for others when experience should tell us that gratitude benefactors are the exception rather than the rule. Parents expect gratitude from their children, but in turn, they do not regularly give them an appropriate example of gratitude to follow. How can children be expected to show gratitude when they do not know what it is? When they see it practiced so seldom that they cannot identify it? As with most children's behaviors, again, the best way to get gratitude is to live it in the example that is set for children. Parents have no right to expect a behavior from their children that they as parents have not yet made a part of their own behavior repertoire.

Martie and her mother, Mrs. E, were clients of mine for three months. Initially just Martie was the client, because Mrs. E made an appointment only for Martie and brought her to my office. Mrs. E presented Martie to me as a "psychological disaster area" and insisted that I: (1) perform an on-the-spot full psychological evaluation, (2) agree with her "disaster area" analysis of Martie, and (3) cure Martie completely in four or fewer weekly visits—in time for them to enjoy the Christmas holidays. At least, Mrs. E did not expect a magic pill or injection to make everything work again.

Not too surprisingly, the first four weeks of seeing mother and daughter were required just to convince Mrs. E that the problem was not solely her daughter's problem. At first, Mrs. E saw no way in which she as a mother might be contributing to what was described as her daughter's most severe problem—that of complete ingratitude for the sacrifices that Mr. and Mrs. E had endured to provide Martie with the finer things in life. After all, why shouldn't Martie express her gratitude? Mrs. E reiterated to Martie hourly what a lucky girl she was, how her parents had given her everything any young girl could ever want, and that she had so much to be thankful for and should, therefore, show her appreciation.

At the same time, I kept looking for Mrs. E to demonstrate just exactly what she *did* want to see in her daughter, but most of what I saw in Mrs. E's behavior when she talked about herself and her situation was how unfairly life, and in particular, her husband and her daughter, had treated her. She was concerned that her husband had changed jobs from a high-paying position with a stable company to a job with a small struggling company where he earned only $18,000 a year. She saw nothing to be grateful for when her husband's job satisfaction had leaped upward in only four weeks.

Mrs. E saw nothing to be thankful for in the fact that Martie had been bringing home consistent B+ report cards for over three years. "Why doesn't she make straight A's?" "She could if she tried." "Why did Mr. E take a twenty percent salary cut just so he could work at something he enjoyed more?" "Why doesn't he understand the inconvenience of trying to stretch the budget to cover the shopping for a family of three?"

Fully seventy percent of the early therapy sessions with Mrs. E served as excellent examples of ingratitude modeling—modeling that her daughter had watched and incorporated faithfully into her own behavioral pattern. It was fortunate that Mrs. E was minimally defensive about her own behavior when I replayed excerpts of two videotaped sessions back to her. At first she was disbelieving, then shocked as she watched herself. Then she became guilt-laden, remorseful, apologetic, and finally determined—determined to practice what she had been preaching to Martie—determined to set a desirable example for her daughter to follow. Mrs. E was not at all convinced that changes in her own behavior would bring about similar changes in her daughter's behavior. And, indeed, no appreciable difference in her nine-year-old's behavior was discernable for six weeks. Then, imagine the surprise on Mrs. E's face when Martie unexpectedly thanked her for making an unscheduled social stop at a friend's house while mother and daughter were returning from taking the family dog to the vet. Then there was the unexpected gratitude voiced by Martie just to tell her mother that she appreciated not being harrassed any more to make straight A's in school. Mrs. E was pleasantly surprised to learn that Martie was still pliable behaviorally and that she, as her mother, could exercise a measure of control over her daughter, even if the control was indirect and produced a somewhat delayed reaction.

Parental Modeling and Drugs

A favorite excuse among teen-agers to justify their use of drugs is the excessive use of drugs they see among their parents. If parents make a big thing out of the beneficial effects of drugs (most often, alcohol, prescription, and over-the-counter drugs are used by parents) the children likewise will tend to develop inappropriately excessive needs for drugs. Occasionally, though, adults will have headaches, upset stomachs, or sleepless nights. Parents who treat these and a hundred other symptoms with aspirin, headache remedies, antacids, tranquilizers, and sleeping pills are giving their teen-agers the excuse they may have been seeking to do some drug experimentation of their own. Children can be told of the benefits of required prescription drugs, when they are used to maintain satisfactory bodily functioning, without stressing a dependence on the medication to obtain a desired feeling or mood. In many cases, where children say they use drugs because their parents drink or take tranquilizers they are merely searching for some justification to make themselves feel less guilty about using drugs. Nevertheless, the parent who emphasizes medication and drug use is what the teen-ager was looking for and will be taken as sufficient reason for self-experimentation. This makes it important for parents to do their part to live healthy, satisfying lives without excessive dependence upon drugs.

I know a set of parents who were astounded when their eighteen-year-old son, J.G., was arrested for possession and sale of marijuana. This boy enjoyed the lift he got from smoking a joint, and he enjoyed seeing his friends indulge as well. His desire to sell marijuana had as much to do with desire for companionship as it did with the meager profits he obtained from the few sales he made.

J.G. saw how his parents had turned more and more to tranquilizers and alcohol as they became increasingly engrained in today's achievement, production, consumption-oriented way of life.

At first, both parents turned to alcohol socially. Then every conceivable event became an excuse for alcohol. It was used to start the day, and a stiff drink was used to cap off an evening. Increased usage of marijuana seemed like no big thing to J.G., because mood-altering drugs were a way of life at his home. Like many other members of his generation, J.G. thought it was arbitrary and unfair that marijuana consumption was illegal. Thus, his motivation for smoking marijuana was fueled from several sources: (1) joints were "in" with his friends, (2) J.G. liked and was beginning to depend psychologically on the lift they gave him, (3) he liked the idea of defying what he considered an unjust law, and (4) foremost, he could see no legitimate complaint that his parents could offer against it because they were far more hooked on alcohol than he was on marijuana.

It goes without saying that J.G.'s parents did not share this reasoning with him. They would have been unable to identify with any of J.G.'s pro-marijuana views, even if J.G. had gone to the trouble of sharing his reasoning with them. All they could think of when the police called to advise them of J.G.'s arrest on charges of possession and sale of marijuana was, "How could our son do such an awful thing to us after all we have done for him. He has shamed us by breaking the law and getting arrested. Where did we go wrong?"

The condemnation of son and selves was severe. Starting the next week, several slow-moving therapy sessions were required to help these parents understand that they had as great a problem with self-control concerning their alcohol usage as did their son with his marijuana. It was not easy for them to admit that they were fallible humans who were capable of errors that were observed by their son, if not by themselves, and were incorporated into his thinking and behavior.

Just as these parents were getting in touch with their fallibility, their son was sentenced to six months in jail—none of which was suspended. The guilt that they loaded on themselves as they began to see their modeling role in the scheme of things was unnecessarily heavy, and more time was required for them to forgive themselves than was required for them to forgive their son.

Visits to their son during imprisonment became increasingly open and served to bring parents and son psychologically closer together. It took the unfortunate event of J.G.'s imprisonment for these parents to get in touch with what had happened to them and to bring their own drinking problems under control.

Showing Appropriate Responses to Life's Events

Parents should let their own reactions to events be of an intensity that fits the occasion. A few parents exhibit inappropriate behavior toward their children by overreacting to situations that are simply aggravating and annoying. Simple events are treated with all the magnitude of a catastrophe. Some parents have been known to then ride right through genuine tragedy with the appearance of being unruffled. In either case, children learn to develop reactions that are appropriate to the occasion by observing appropriate behavior exemplified by their parents. Consider the following example:

>Mr. J purchased a new compact car and obtained great satisfaction in telling friends it got thirty six miles per gallon on the highway and could go from zero to fifty miles per hour in only 8.4 seconds. He announced to Mrs. J and their twelve-year-old-daughter, Julie, that is was time to confirm the zero to fifty statistic. He was willing to bet he could go from zero to fifty in eight seconds flat or maybe even 7.9. He made a point of taking the entire family with him as he headed out to a seldom-used, two-block section of a nearby street.
>
>Julie was excited about the possibility of being a first-hand observer of squealing tires, burning rubber, and thundering smoke, but her mother wanted no part of the one-man drag race. Mr. J was quick to point out that his planned experiment was not a drag race, but rather, a performance test. As Julie and Mr. J arrived at the scene, he was pleased to see the dry pavement and no traffic around. Mr. J decided to let Julie have the thrill of confirming the car's performance.
>
>When the second hand was straight up, she gave the signal, and Mr. J's right foot hit the accelerator with the impact of a bullet. There were squealing tires, boiling smoke, and a thunderous roar. Julie, too, felt the excitement as their speed picked up, then suddenly her father yelled "Now," and she knew the car had reached fifty miles per hour as she carefully observed the second hand. Mr. J said, "OK, let's hear it. What was the time?" as he braked to a halt at the curb. Hesitating, Julie said, "Uh, Daddy I think it was just a speck under ten seconds."
>
>"What!" he shouted. "No Way! You blew it! We'll check it again!"
>
>As the red-faced Mr. J wheeled the car around for another run, he again carefully detailed the time instructions to his now slightly frightened daughter. He reiterated the importance of her signaling him when the second hand was straight up as well as the importance of her noting the second hand's exact position at the instant he called out "Fifty." Again the car was put through its paces with the accompanying noise and smoke. As Mr. J excitedly screamed, "Fifty," Julie's eyes were glued to the second hand. She said, "Got it —10.1 seconds."

"What?" he yelled. "Impossible. I'll have to get someone who can tell time accurately and do it all over again another day." There were several other tries, first with Julie's mother, then with Julie and Mrs. J, and then with the ultimate clocker—an electronic stopwatch. The scene became more traumatic each time Mr. J demanded that his family accompany him to the test track. The stop watch did not earn its expensive price. After four trials the times still ranged from 9.6 to 10.1 seconds. This was a disgrace to Mr. J, and he felt it was time to let the car dealer know about it. This he did promptly.

It never had occurred to Mr. J that acceleration was only one aspect of performance, or that he had failed to investigate the thirty-six miles-per-gallon claim. He also seemed to disregard the fact that the car started easily, was dependable transportation for getting to and from work, needed no repairs, and did get sufficient gasoline mileage to give the family's tight budget a needed breather. The monthly payments were not easy to meet, but this did not seem to cause Mr. J any particular alarm.

At the car dealer, Mr. J insisted to the shop foreman that the car was advertised to go from zero to fifty in 8.4 seconds and he intended to see that the car stayed in the shop until it met this performance standard. Finally, four days later, Mr. J was called to the shop and taken for a test drive with stopwatch in hand and daughter Julie in the back seat. This time Mr. J was satisfied—8.3, 8.4, and 8.2 seconds were the speeds. The car's acceleration was now as good as or better than the advertised figure.

Mr. J had never been particularly bothered by the fact that his car was advertised to get thirty-six miles per gallon as well, but had actually never gotten over thirty-one. Now, after the extensive motor tuning to obtain the improved acceleration, Mr. J found the mileage was down to nineteen-miles-per-gallon. This still did not trouble him. His struggling young family needed to get on its feet, but the car's lack of mileage economy seemed to make no impression on him at all. The weekly budget was again attacked to come up with the extra dollars needed to purchase gasoline to do the same amount of driving as before.

The J family car had always had enough acceleration to pull into traffic or to pass other cars as needed, thus Mr. J's emphasis on acceleration served as inappropriate modeling for Julie. The more important issue of obtaining sufficient gasoline economy to make the family budget stretch from week to week was skirted—again modeling behavior and attitude inappropriate to the family's financial need.

Teen-agers: Primary Models for Other Teen-Agers

Teen-agers invest a great deal of time following behavior that is exhibited by their peers. One behavior that teen-age children learn early on is the fear of adverse criticism from significant others—the fear of looking bad, the fear of failure, and the fear of being inadequate through the eyes of others hangs particularly heavy over this age group.

Teen-agers especially are afraid of being laughed at by their peers. The significant persons in most teen-agers lives are their peers. This comes about because the average teen-ager is in a stage of transition from child to adult. When a teen-ager feels the particular need to be more adult, he or she may find it necessary to act increasingly venturesome, which is threatening in itself. When the would-be adult demonstrates what he or she thinks is adult behavior that goes wrong (either as perceived by self or others), there is a tremendous loss of face and a feeling of regret over having asserted oneself in front of so many persons who are important.

This is what happened to Hal as he overheard the last of a conversation at school in which Debbie had just turned down a ballgame date with Emory. Hal saw this as an opportunity to get a ballgame date for himself, as well as the perfect chance to demonstrate his advanced date-getting skills in front of several friends and some older students he wanted to impress. He sauntered up to Debbie and said, "Hey Debbie, you couldn't go to the game with Emory because you're saving yourself for me Friday night. Right?" "Wrong!" answered Debbie, as she turned away with a toss of her blonde hair toward her next class. The students to whom Hal was going to teach a lesson a moment earlier thought it was the funniest thing since comic books even though Hal was crushed. He had ventured and lost. He had seen other boys do it, but somehow the behavior he had learned from them did not work for him, and he, in turn, had failed to carry out the adult action he wanted to in front of his peers. One hopes that Hal learned enough by this temporary failure to improve his chances with Debbie on a later occasion.

Do parents have a right to be concerned about the kind of behavior that their teen-agers pick up from fellow teen-agers? Yes. But whoever a child selects as friends to emulate and model behavior from is his or her own decision.

If parents have been able to make favorable input into their children's lives without alienating them, they can expect to make further favorable input regarding their teen-ager's selection of peers.

In fact, where parents have made their favorable influence felt, little new input will be necessary in regard to selection of a child's friends, because the child will have a tendency to migrate to peers who act as favorable role models.

But what if a mother and father do not have any appreciable degree of influence over a teen-ager? What if their teen-ager has not grasped their subtle clues about choice of friends? What if the parents fear that their child may develop undesirable behaviors they have observed among their child's friends? If the child will discuss the issue, it is time to halt the subtle clues and initiate open discussion of the situation. The parents will want to list the reasons that make them perceive an individual or group as a poor choice. At this point, they should try to understand what their child gains from the friendship. Parents should then ask for and listen to their child's feelings about attributes and drawbacks of the friendship.

For a time, parents may be able to put enough restrictions and restraints on their children to make it very difficult for them to interact with anyone they disapprove of. Still, no parent can continuously restrict a child forever. At some point in a child's life, parents will no longer be able to choose "good company." When this point is reached, children will smoke pot, drink alcohol and have premarital sex if they wish. Before this point is reached, we can only hope that parents have learned to back off with regard to the restrictive controls they try to impose. Parents can gradually replace their need for control and protection of their children with open trust. When parents exhibit trust toward their children, they can expect their children to trust them in return and to be more receptive to parental ideas concerning, among other things, choice of friends.

Trust

Self-trust must come before trust of others. Others cannot be trusted until one first trusts oneself. It is difficult for an individual to trust others in a given situation when one has little self-trust in comparable situations. It is easy for parents to distrust their children and impute their own feelings of temptation and guilt onto them as they contemplate their children's motives in a given set of circumstances. After all, the parents were once youngsters, too.

Thus, parents come up with an uneasy feeling that could best be called distrust, although a majority of parents would quickly deny that they distrust their children. In many cases, children have no appreciable conscious awareness of distrust on the part of their parents. Yet distrust does influence children at an unconscious level. It results in children feeling that they need to act differently when they are away from their parents. This feeling of not being trusted can lead to behavior in the parents' absence that is based on the principle of self-fulfilling prophecy. The very thing a parent dreads and fears is what the child feels somehow compelled to do. Self-fulfilling prophecy has a way of bringing the parents' greatest worries crashing down onto their heads. If the child is aware of the feeling of being distrusted, he or she may rationalize by thinking, "Well, my parents think that I'm doing it, and they accuse me of doing it, so I had might as well be doing it and enjoying whatever fun I can get from it." This has a way not of disappointing the parents' worst dreads and fears, but rather, of insuring that the parental fears are realized.

But what if a parent still has a genuine lack of trust and still fears what a child might do in the parent's absence? Or perhaps the parent has accurate information from a dependable source regarding a child's undesirable behavior. A mother and father could discuss whether or not they share the same fear about the child. If they both hold some intense fear, they should approach their teen-ager with their fear, as well as with any available facts. They might openly tell their child why they hold this fear, and they could express the undesirable developments they think could result from the feared behavior. The child may be surprised and even flattered at their concern. The teen-ager will be grateful for the parents' direct and open approach to their fear (although this may not be apparent in the child's attitude and behavior) as opposed to the usual accusations, implications, and strange negative parental messages that might have occurred. A child may act uninterested in the parents' concern, but will nevertheless be taking in the conversation. A child may also act uninterested when discussing parent-child conflicts or expectations, but one may rest assured that the parents' verbalizations are heard and perceived by the child. It would be too much for a child to admit to appreciating parents' concerns; parents should not expect this. Children feel it is necessary to act as if such discussions are beneath them; they want parents and others to think of them as adults—adults being people who do not need negative feedback about their behavior.

Parents may as well trust their children, because all the distrust and restrictiveness in the world will not keep them out of trouble, if trouble is in the offing. Parents who let their teen-agers know where they stand as parents, what they expect, and that they believe their children will live up to their expectations increase the chances of their trust being justified. Of course, it goes without saying that parents' expectations must be realistic and attainable. If the child feels the expectations are absurd, the expectations will be treated that way.

Get Trust by Giving It

The most desirable way to raise trustworthy children is first to trust them. Parents would do well to trust them at all ages and behave toward them with trust. Emerson's wise words on this subject can only be improved by substituting the word *children* for *men*. He said "Trust men and they will be true to you; treat them greatly and they will show themselves great." If we expect our children to trust us, to trust our experience and judgement, to trust others, and especially to trust themselves, we must show them trust by first being trusting and trustworthy parents.

Ventilating Strong Feelings

As children enter their teen-age years, parents will begin to reap the pay offs of past trust they have shown toward their children. It is completely appropriate for parents at this point to describe their expectations about sex, drugs, smoking, and drinking to their children. If the parents feel strongly about these matters, it is desirable that they talk with their children about it. More precisely, it is the obligation of strongly opinionated parents to let their thinking be known to their children, rather than to become martyrs by stifling their own strong feelings. There is no reason why parents cannot have strong feelings, and there is not reason for them not to share their strong feelings with their children as well as with each other. When strong feelings are ventilated in a concerned, caring, supportive manner, there is no cause for parents to feel guilty if they display temper in the course of explaining their views. A show of temper is an unconscious, or perhaps conscious, controlling maneuver designed to get one's own way. At times, certain parents have been known unjustly to use the temper tantrum technique to try to control their children, although we usually think, and rightfully so, of the temper tantrum technique as a ploy reserved just for children.

5
Respect:
A Give-and-Take Affair

"My children don't respect me." How many times have you heard that statement from a disappointed parent? As with communication, respect is a two-way street. To earn respect from others, especially one's own children, it is necessary first to give respect.

Giving respect represents a large portion of the necessary process of *earning* respect. And sustained respect must be earned, because it is not automatically assigned to parents just because they are the so-called heads of the household. Being given this measure of authority carries no special meaning or measure of respect from children. Concerned parents who work hard to be respected citizens in their community often need to redirect a portion of their concern for being respected toward their children.

What is Respect?

Children need parents' respect. This statement sounds reasonable enough, but what is respect? Respect is a set of attitudes and behaviors that exemplify a positive regard and recognition of the rights of another person.

Should parents just tell their children how much they respect them and be done with it? An explicit confirmation of respect is not necessary, because children know when they are respected. Perhaps some young children do not know what the word *respect* means, but one can rest assured that they can understand and discuss the concept intelligently when it is presented on their level.

Freedom to Speak: A Measure of Respect

One might further answer some of these questions by asking still another one: Do I as a parent often interrupt my children when they are speaking? Parents who interrupt their children frequently and who otherwise dominate conversations with them are in fact disrespectful of their children's constitutional right to free speech. Let us consider still one more question: How often do I tell the children to shut up, a statement that is usually followed by, "It's so noisy around here that I can't think?" The wording may vary in individual cases because there are several ways to transmit this negative disrespectful message, but the message to children is always the same: What you are saying is unimportant, childish gibberish. Parents have learned a lesson in respect when they allow children to finish their thoughts after they have started to speak—that is, assuming the children have not themselves interrupted another ongoing conversation. When parents can successfully function in this manner, they then have reason to expect that their children will allow them the opportunity to finish speaking after having started a new sentence or thought.

Children too young to verbalize a definition for respect can nevertheless tell of specific events in their recent past in which they were made to feel good about themselves. There will be occasions when these events involve one or both parents and something they have done to indicate that they care for their children's opinions, feelings, or rights. A very young child may demonstrate his or her grasp of the concept of respect by saying, "Mommy [Daddy] makes me feel good when she [he]————."

Children, especially young children, do not readily understand that what parents have to say may be more important than what they as children have to say. Most young children are not ready to consider that anyone's ideas have more interest or urgency than their own.

Above all, parents would do well to try to avoid the power tactic of telling a child that what he or she has to say is not important, or that it may best go unsaid. Statements of this type would be clearly labelled as disrespectful if they were conveyed from one adult to another adult. It is time to set aside the double standard of respect, in which we have one standard for adults and a more rigid standard for children. Whenever a child is told explicitly or implicitly that his or her message is not important, the child is reminded that what he or she was thinking was not worthy of presenting for the consideration of others. Children whose conversational input repeatedly receives such a parental squelch will lose some respect for the parent, as they should. But more important, these children lose respect for the value of their own ideas and thought processes.

The old saying, "Children should be seen and not heard," should be put in the round file where it belongs and supplanted with a new one, "Children should be seen *and* heard."

Parents need to find time to listen to their children's questions, to respect their inquisitiveness, and to answer them as truthfully as possible. If a parent is not sure of an answer, it is best to come out clearly and just say so. This need not cause a parent's ego to sink. What many parents fail to appreciate is the simple fact that a child does not lose respect for a parent who simply admits he or she does not understand something or does not know the answer to a question. Perhaps the best way to win a child's respect is to stick with the truth in every conversation—even if the truth means admitting that you cannot answer a child's question.

A World of Knees and Ankles

Being a child means living in a world of knees and ankles. In addition to being physically shorter than the adults in their world, most children also feel they are greatly outnumbered. Unfortunately, as children grow, many adults in their environment continue to give them knee-and-ankle responses that serve to make them feel like kindergarten-age children. Parents should make every effort to avoid this, and should also discourage such treatment of their children by other adults.

In addition, it is time parents stopped talking about their children to other adults when the children are present or within hearing distance. What more effective knee-and-ankle response can be made than a negative statement about oneself spoken to a third party in one's presence. When such conversations occur, children are usually soaking up all that is said, although they may give the appearance of not perceiving the conversation at all. Most adult friends and associates have enough respect not to talk about us with others when we are present, and children surely deserve this same respect. If parents do find it necessary to talk about their children's behavior with someone—and parents might do well to honor their children's privacy in the same way they honor that of adults—they would do well to respect the child enough to do their talking when the child is not present.

Self-Fulfilling Prophecy

The laws of self-fulfilling prophecy are strong; parents cannot get away with heaping negative generalizations upon their children without producing some harmful backlash effects. Self-fulfilling prophecy is what happens when we repeatedly predict what someone will do until the point is reached that they begin to believe it and accept it as fact. Often in self-fulfilling prophecy we set up circumstances and environmental variables in a way that increases the probability of the prophecy's fulfillment. As children begin to believe in their parents' predictions about them, their behavior is modified in such a way as to bring about the predicted event. For example, when children are repeatedly told that they are bad and cannot be trusted, they begin, at some point, to believe this about themselves. Self-fulfilling prophecy is one of the more dangerous weapons that unknowing parents have in their arsenal of child-defeating techniques. Negative prophetic statements about one's own children during the formative years indicate a callous disrespect for the child's attributes and self-concept.

Following are some all-encompassing, generalized, negative statements; they could be called negative self-fulfilling prophecies, or "knee and ankle" put-down statements. "Girl, you don't do enough work around this house to break the Sabbath." "Listen, kid, it's time you pulled your weight around here. What you do isn't enough to earn the salt that goes into your bread." "Bad grades again. You're just like your father's side—dumb." "I know you're out smoking pot every day after school before I get in from work." "I can see it now. Why you are going to grow up to be—nothing but a common criminal." "Can't you ever do anything right?" "Must I do everything for you?"

Courtesy: An Ingredient of Respect

A large part of respect is represented by simple courtesy. Erastus Wiman aptly said the following of courtesy: "Nothing is ever lost by courtesy. It is the cheapest of pleasures; costs nothing and conveys much. It pleases him who gives and him who receives, and thus, like mercy, is twice blessed." If this be the case, and I definitely think it is, why do parents use courtesy so sparingly with their children? Perhaps they perceive courtesy as giving in to the children or as a potential threat to their supposedly superior role as parents. Some parents probably perceive courteous behavior toward their children as weakening the position of strength derived from being adults, which could then lead to situations permitting the children to take advantage of them.

Yet parents can practice courtesy toward their children without granting the children's every wish. Parents have the capability of speaking up to their children with a firm but friendly no when it is called for. A friendly, matter-of-fact no shows respect for a child's feelings at the same time that it sets limits on the child's behavior. Perhaps working parents could learn how to be courteous to their children by interacting with them as they would with their co-workers. The same courtesy and tone of voice are equally as appropriate for one's children as they are for one's co-workers. There is no good reason why parents cannot experience the double blessing described by Wiman in their relationships with their own children.

A seemingly small thing, such as knocking before entering a child's room, shows respect for the child's privacy; it is a small courtesy that conveys a big meaning about privacy and could easily be part of any family's standard operating procedure. The child is then more likely to honor the parents' privacy.

As a friend and I watched Saturday afternoon football on his television, I could not help over hearing an incident between his wife and daughter in the adjoining living room. The daughter had been practicing the piano about ten minutes when her mother came into the room and said, "How about letting me practice a while." The mother did not wait for an answer or even slow down as she gathered her music together and headed for the piano bench, adjusting the lamp on the way. The mother had phrased her statement in question form as if to ask permission to use the piano, but had not actually waited for a reply. The daughter really had no prerogative—no decision to make—except to relinquish the piano to her mother.

The daughter did the only thing she felt she could do. She got up and politely left the room. But what message really came through to her? One can rest assured it was not, "I think I will let Mother practice now, and I really appreciate her being nice enough to ask." The message was more likely to be, "Mother thinks my practice and musical career are not as important as hers," or "Mother acts as if she's being respectful by asking before she bulldozes me away from the piano." The daughter might think, "Why didn't mother just come out and order me to leave? It would have had the same effect. I wonder what would have happened if I had told her I needed to finish my practice session first and that she could use the piano when I was through?" But the daughter had a pretty good idea of how the mother would react to that, so she assumed a subservient role and withdrew from any conflict by withdrawing from the room.

If Mother really had such an urgent need to play the piano, she might have said, "I really must practice for the wedding I'm playing for tomorrow. This is the only time I have because I must go to church and practice with the soloist in thirty minutes. You can practice all you wish after I leave." On the other hand, if the mother's situation were different and her need to practice less urgent, she could have phrased the question as she actually did and then waited for a reply, or she could have asked, "When will you be through practicing? I need to practice soon, but it can wait if you will be finished reasonably soon." In a situation without urgency, the mother could have said something like, "I need to practice when you are finished. Do you think I'll have time to clear the table and wash dishes before you are finished with the piano?" Any of these replies would have shown appropriate respect both for the daughter and for the mother's desire to practice fairly soon.

Excessive Kidding: A Form of Disrespect

Like adults children fear scorn and being laughed at. It is time adults recognize that children do not like being the butt of jokes any more than adults do. Adults who kid teen-agers and belittle matters that are serious to them have found an excellent way to erode any mutual respect that might have existed between them, as well as a way to widen the generation gap. Teen-agers will tell you quickly that most teasing concerns dating and their relationships with friends of the opposite sex, areas they are especially sensitive about anyway. In the value system of the older teen-ager, dating is exceedingly important, but too often, adults in the child's environment make such concerns seem foolish and trivial.

The feelings of teen-agers can also be respected by keeping silent in front of their friends about the cute little things they did when they were toddlers. It is very embarrassing for teen-agers when their parents relate these anecdotes to significant others in their lives. The business of making children the brunt of jokes has no place in a family relationship where the parties involved expect respect.

My Name: More Than a Means of Identification

Respect also appears any time we regard and treat persons as individuals and accord them an identity all their own. One can do this with all persons, adults and children alike, by addressing them with the name of *their* choice. Persons should be called the name they want to be called. It costs nothing to use the given name, nickname, or title that an individual prefers. Any nickname that parents use for a child should be one of the child's choosing—certainly not a nickname adopted by the parents against the child's wishes. It is appropriate to call a child by the name he or she prefers, even if the chosen name differs from the name given the child at the time of birth. Children sometimes go through stages of adopting nicknames they find attractive. Even though the names are often dropped along the way, parents should exhibit respect for the child's preferences. Parents set examples of disrespect when they call a child derogatory names such as Bean Brain, Pinhead, Scaredy Cat, Pee Wee, Knucklehead, Numbskull, Dumbell, Cry Baby, or Nitwit. Children who have been called one of these names most of their lives may begin to assume a portion of the role assigned to that name as they begin to fulfill the prophecy of the name.

Just how important is a child's name? Exceedingly important, and I offer the following example as proof. Our son decided he would streamline his three-speed bike, to make it faster by removing all unnecessary, nonfunctional weight. First went the chain guard (this has had its effect on the grease content of his right trouser leg). Next went the fenders, weighing all of twelve ounces each. As trim and seemingly functional parts were removed in the name of efficiency, it became apparent that three items would stay until the end. These were metal identification tags made along the lines of automobile license plates, which he had attached to the bicycle seat. The name plates represented three states, Georgia, Tennessee, and North Carolina, but they had one thing in common. They all had his name, Richard, printed in large letters. A lot of things could be stripped from the bicycle, but his name was not one of them. His identity and his identification with the bicycle were to be maintained at all costs.

As seen by this example, all children have a strong need for an identity, and parents who do not know their child's preferred name identity have their work cut out for them. And parents who know their child's preferred identity but have not gotten around to using it also have their work cut out. Parents who wish to call their child by a name other than the child's choice might stop and ask themselves why it is so important to them. They might also ask to what extent they can expect to exercise identity control over the child fifteen years from now.

How Parents Earn Disrespect

Respect is neither earned nor given by parents who are repeatedly overpermissive with their children. Conversely, parents show respect for a child when they place a higher value on making positive input into the child's value system than they do on keeping temporary peace in the family by giving in to the child's unreasonable whim. By setting reasonable limits as opposed to allowing complete overpermissiveness, parents demonstrate a needed degree of self-respect by not discarding their own thinking in the face of opposition by a demanding child. More will be said about setting limits in Chapter 9, "What to Expect of Whom."

Parents frequently earn disrespect when they make promises to their children that they either do not intend to carry out or may have no available means to carry out. A parent may be able temporarily to alleviate a persistently begging child by promising to do some desired thing at a future time. But guess again if you are trusting that the child will forget it thus letting you off the hook. No elephant can match the memory of a child carrying an unfulfilled parental promise. As a safe guide, it is desirable to make promises to children only when the promised event can definitely be delivered and when there is a definite intention to deliver.

When there is intent to fulfill a child's request, but the ingredient of assurance of ability to deliver is missing, the uncertainty of the situation can be shared with a child. It is all right to tell a child of your wish to comply with a request if, at the same time, you cite the contingencies and possible circumstances that might prevent your being able to follow through. Situations involving intent to comply but uncertainty of fulfillment are more readily accepted by school-age children who trust their parents. Younger children are not as capable of understanding an abstract conditional intention. Furthermore, children who have not learned to trust their parents will have trouble believing their parents' stated desire to meet their request. So it is wise to use this technique only after you have developed a trusting relationship.

Another sure way to kill a child's respect is the use of threats as behavior controllers. The parent who often threatens punishment and seldom delivers earns disrespect. The child learns to pay no attention when the parent threatens, because instead of the promised negative consequence for the child, the parent comes back with another threat when the child's undesirable behavior reappears. Why should a child respect what a parent says when neither the promised desired event not the promised (threatened) undesired event ever takes place?

Self-Respect: An Indispensible Ingredient

What is self-respect? It is nothing but a healthy acceptance of oneself, complete with an awareness of one's strengths and weaknesses and past history of successes and failures. Self-respect allows one to build on past successes and to learn from past failures without becoming haughty over the former or wiped out over the latter.

How do children learn self-respect? The easiest way is by living with parents who respect themselves, their children, their neighbors, and their co-workers. Children who have observed their parents experiencing success and failure with equanimity—who have watched their parents deal with joy and disappointment with determination—will benefit by developing a deep sense of self-respect on their own.

Parents who count their own ideas and opinions equivalent to those of others are giving their children a lesson in self-respect. Parents who put undue emphasis on what others say or on "what will the neighbors think" are showing disrespect for their own thinking. They tend to raise children who also overemphasize the business of pleasing others at their own expense.

Children soon learn to value their own thinking when they are fortunate enough to have parents who value their children's ideas and opinions. Pre-school and elementary school children place value on what they see being valued by their parents—in this case, their selves, their ideas, and their opinions.

Self-respect also comes from a healthy respect for the skills and accomplishments of others without feeling resentment or dispair in seeing others excel. Genuine self-respect does not wane at seeing the successes of another. Again, children learn this aspect of self-respect most readily by seeing it exemplified by their parents. Parents ought also to be alert to their children's strivings and aspirations so they can help their children maintain a sense of self-worth, especially when sought-after goals are not attained or praiseworthy achievements are not forthcoming with regularity. Self-respect is the platform needed for the launching of respect for others.

6
Who Makes the Decisions?

Have you ever entered a house for the first time and wondered, "Who runs this home?" The question is easily answered in a home with a baby; you will find that nine times out of ten, the baby runs the home. But who decides when a parent will jump up and run to the infant's side? Who decides when it is mealtime, when mealtime is over, when it is time to be changed? The baby decides, that's who.

Babies learn early that crying allows them to exercise great control over their parents. Practically all of a mother's time and much of father's time is occupied in supplying a baby's needs. Whenever a baby feels a bit uncomfortable or wants something, a few yells usually suffice to get the required attention. A great many babies, as well as some older children, often train their parents in this manner, and before long, one or both parents are performing as if they were trained laboratory mice. Yet this inappropriate parental behavior often prevents parents from serving a useful parental function, that of decision-maker.

Computer Mothers

Perhaps you have seen a mother who is more or less "programmed" in much the same way that a computer is programmed. The children, no longer infants, have only to verbalize what they expect of mother, and mother does the rest. These frequent inappropriate requests are equivalent to placing a deck of punched instruction cards in a computer and pushing the start button. Lights flash, wheels whirl, and gears turn as the mother, a human computer, goes into a flurry of action to meet her children's demands. She feels she must make sure they have everything that they desire. She feels she must function efficiently in a businesslike manner to make certain the children are not deprived of any of the childhood things they are "supposed" to have. Nothing but the best will suffice for her children as she tries to be a "good" mother. The mother must ensure that in later life her adult children will never be able to look back and lament that they wanted for anything. This method also insures that a mother can never be made to feel guilty about how she raised her children because she gave them her all. Her children had whatever they wanted regardless of her personal sacrifice.

Unfortunately, many parents do not realize that this kind of parental behavior is completely unnecessary. Such one-way giving on the part of either parent has no place in child-rearing and is not necessarily associated with being a good parent. When parents function with such a great need to be needed, they delay the time when their children can become involved in developing their own decision-making skills. In fact, children have no need to learn decision-making skills so long as their responsibility-assumers, parents, are around.

Make Your Own Decisions

Adults fail to use their own minds when they allow others to do their thinking and decision-making for them. When parents abdicate responsibility they increase the chance that their children will add this unfortunate parental characteristic to their own behavior repertoires.

The tables can also be turned when adults never let children make their own decisions. Many people assume that a person who acts confident knows more about what is going on than they know themselves. Of course, this is not necessarily true. When our teen-agers learn always to respect the judgment of others over their own judgment, they become overly sensitive to the thinking of their peers. This natural tendency for teen-agers to be inordinately influenced by the opinions of their peers is given an unnecessary boost by parents who do not respect their children's opinions, parents who fail to encourage children to become involved in decisions that affect their daily life.

A large proportion of the adult population goes along with the thinking of the crowd in order to keep cherished friendships functioning smoothly. Adults, too, often underestimate their ability to interject original, novel ideas into conversations for fear of making enemies of the significant others in their lives. It seems safer and is often easier to remain mute, thus allowing a viable and possibly better alternative suggestion to go unmentioned and thus unconsidered. By not going against the wishes of those whose favor they want to cultivate, adults can avoid feeling that their interpersonal relationships are threatened. A piece of a better world is sacrificed in the name of maintaining temporary harmony.

Children, especially teen-agers who are prone to following role models, latch on to this peace-at-any-price behavior. Because making new friends outside the family is of great importance for practically all teen-agers, they sometimes play their roles as group conformers better than their adult counterparts from which they learned. This is exemplified by teen-agers who are overly sensitive to what their peers think of them, teen-agers who are too threatened by the loss of precarious friendships to think for themselves.

As adults, we need to believe in ourselves and in our own good thinking. In addition, we need to exemplify attitudes for our children that will cause them to realize that automatically conforming to the majority opinion sometimes leads to wrong decisions and ill-advised actions.

The Decision-Making Process

Why do parents and teen-agers alike spend so much time and energy worrying about problems and decisions to be made? One of the central reasons for worry and intimidation by self-generated fear is the lack of objective information about a problem. Quite often, initial information is only partially accurate and is usually incomplete as well. This is all the more reason to get the needed facts for decision-making, even if those facts are not pleasant to hear. The facts still exist in any event— even if we are ignorant of them. When we apprise ourselves of the facts, we are in a position to respond based on this knowledge in a manner that will either take advantage of an opportunity or lessen the impact of a misfortune.

Method in Scientific Decision-Making

One of the best ways to structure the decision-making process is to use the scientific method. It need not be restricted to professional scientists. All adults, especially parents, can benefit from this process because everyone has an opportunity to apply it daily in his or her life. The skills involved in the process of scientific decision-making merit being handed down from generation to generation. Youth will learn to apply this technique more quickly if they see it practiced by their parents. The steps in scientific decision-making briefly are:

1. Gather available information.
2. Formulate the problem.
3. Secure missing pertinent information.
4. Analyze the facts.
5. Establish the alternatives
6. Decide: select the most desirable alternative.
7. Follow through with determination.
8. Assess the outcome.

An elaboration of these steps follows:

Step 1: Gather available information: The importance of this phase of the decision-making process has already been mentioned. It is useful to label information as being either subjective or objective. The objective information can properly be labeled as facts while the subjective can be labeled as perceptions. Both types of information are valuable and should be considered. Information can be secured from a wide variety of sources. One's own children serve as a valuable resource when making family decisions.

Step 2: Formulate the problem: In the process of stating the problem, it is important to be alert to the possibility that there is no problem. In addition, there is usually a possible way of stating the problem that may help by shedding more light on it. If it is confirmed that a genuine problem exists, it needs to be stated, or at least conceptualized, in a concise manner that makes the problem readily recognizable and distinguishable from separate but related problems as much as possible. In fact, the primary problem, as opposed to secondary problems, should be identified. Secondary problems are recognized by the fact that they are frequently stated with a touch of solution in them. A true primary problem can be reduced to its lowest common denominator and stated in simple terms. A primary problem for a young mother might be, "I need less child-rearing interference from my husband's parents." A secondary counterpart to this problem might read, "I need to move from this city because my mother-in-law butts in." The wording in the secondary version of the problem precludes several viable alternatives and necessitates leaving town.

Step 3: Secure missing pertinent information: This step is similar to Step 1 in that subjective and objective information are gathered; however, after the problem has been clearly formulated, obvious information gaps will begin to appear in the data. Also, in this second round of information-gathering, the search is more deliberate as specific bits of information that are strictly pertinent to the concisely formulated problem are sought.

Step 4: Analyze the facts: In scientific decision-making, facts need to be assessed as objectively as possible—even in a detached manner much as an attorney might view the circumstances in a case to be presented in court. As facts are analyzed, it is useful to ask, "How will each of these facts affect the desired final situation?" An alternate way to state this is "Where am I now? Where do I want to be?" More than one satisfactory final situation may come to mind and each, in turn, must be carefully evaluated.

Step 5: Establish the alternatives. The preceeding step flows naturally into this step, in which alternate approaches to a solution are identified. The most satisfactory final solution is more likely to be obtained if several alternatives are considered before any final one is selected. Always try to list as many alternatives as possible. Decision-makers frequently limit their thinking, which results in adopting second- and third-best solutions that are in step with custom and habit.

Step 6: Decide by selecting the most desirable alternative: Too many individuals make this the most important, if not the only, step in problem-solving. Often only one solution has been considered, and the decision involves a choice between attempting this solution or learning to live with the problem. Still others reach this point and freeze, because the possibility of selecting the wrong alternative is quite real, and such persons tend to read catastrophe into any wrong decision.

If all the steps outlined in the decision-making process are followed, there is a high probability that the best alternative will indeed be selected, and that no one could have made a better decision, certainly not without the benefit of hindsight.

The fear of making a wrong decision can have devastating power and can even cause indecision. Some people cannot bear thinking they have made a mistake. Yet, indecision is in truth a very real decision; it is a decision not to decide; it is a decision to give in to a problem.

Step 7: Follow through with determination: This is a step in the decision-making process in which a great many people fumble. Again, the ever-present possibility of failure, fear of the opposition, whether it be in the form of people or circumstances, and the fear of criticism from others all contribute to fumbling a decision before the final goal of problem resolution has been reached. If care has gone into making a decision, the decision should be put into action without rumination about what might have been or what disaster might still loom ahead. Only two things should ever cause a decision alternative to be dropped or reconsidered; they are considered in the final step.

Step 8: Assess the outcome: When the solution goal is reached, it is desirable to review the decision-making process that led to the goal to determine what critical aspects contributed to the success. A review of goal-attainment behavior can be especially useful because it can be added to one's fund of knowledge and can be drawn upon in future decision-making situations.

There are only two valid reasons for altering or dropping a problem-solving decision before the entire decision has been implemented: (1) new information that was not available during the information-gathering steps is found to be inconsistent with the information used for the decision-making, and (2) feedback from the implementation of the selected alternative is unexpected and indicates that further implementation of the present course of action will not result in reaching the desired goal. The first reason is quite different from doing a rehash of the original, unchanged information, and the second reason is quite different from giving up at the first sign of resistance or temporary failure.

Parental Power Masquerading as Decision-Making

Have you seen children who seem to be always pleading for this or that privilege from their parents? It is interesting to observe these children and their parents interactions. Here is a typical case:

Elizabeth was a seventeen-year old high school junior from a two-car, middle-income family. After a Sunday church picnic, the men of the church were enjoying themselves in conversation, but Elizabeth and a couple of her teen-age friends sat nearby looking restless. Soon Elizabeth sheepishly approached her father in a subordinate manner. She timidly asked him for the keys to the car so she could visit some school friends. Her father continued to talk with the other men as if he had not heard her. After a pause, she restated her request, which now contained a note of pleading. Eventually, her father responded, saying, "You don't need the car. You see too much of those people now." I began to get the feeling that this little game had been played before between her and her father. Elizabeth kept trying. After a few more requests, all of which were met with negative implications from her father, it was clear that reward was around the corner. Finally came the inevitable, "Well, OK. This time. But don't go anywhere else and don't stay out past 9 P.M. And this is the last time. Don't ask me any more."

One might think that reinforcing such goal-oriented persistence in a child would be an admirable trait, and it could well be. But what was reinforced here was begging and pleading behavior directed toward getting one's own way. Later in life, if this self-serving, pleading behavior is transferred to other situations involving nonfamily members, this person will be met with stronger resistance and may have real problems in interpersonal relationships.

Situations such as the scene just described also function to give parents a sense of power and authority—a sense of being in control. They nourish their self-image at the expense of their child's self-image. This kind of controlling behavior helps the parent maintain an "I'm up here, you're down there" type of relationship. The father, as well as the daughter in this case, both knew that she would be given the car from the start, but only after she had played the role of a subservient, respectful child. She was made to jump through the hoop, so to speak, just like a trained circus animal, before she could obtain the reward. Was anything constructive accomplished by this unfortunate scene in the presence of outsiders? Actually, no decision-making took place since she and her father both knew that her wish would be eventually granted. Policies about subjects such as the use of the family car could best be worked out at home where the parties were free from public embarrassment and the ears of strangers.

If Elizabeth's father had thought a yes was in order, the following scene could have transpired immediately after her original request:

FATHER: Do you think you can arrange to be back by 4:30?
ELIZABETH: Yes, that's plenty of time.
FATHER: OK—and the right rear tire needs air. There should be a station open close by.
ELIZABETH: Thanks, I'll stop at the station across from the shopping center.
FATHER: Be sure to have a good time.

But what if a no was in order on this occasion? It would be so much better if Elizabeth's father had called her aside to save her from the embarrassment of being turned down in front of strangers. The conversation could take several turns at this point, but it should hinge primarily on the father's reasons for not honoring the request. If the father's reasons are not legitimate, or if the daughter can satisfy his objections, the question should be reconsidered and a yes given. Children deserve to know why parents' decisions that effect them are made. And such reasons must be presented on a level that children can understand. With some practice, parents can learn to empathize with their children and begin to understand how they feel. It is sometimes useful to tell the child that, at another time or under other conditions, the request could be granted. Perhaps the parent's need for the car at the requested time takes priority over the child's needs in a particular instance. There is nothing wrong with mentioning this to the teen-ager in a matter-of-fact manner. When refusing a request, it might be useful to state another time when the request could be granted.

Overgeneralization: Decisions Without Fact

Generalizing about children leads some parents to believe that once a certain type of behavior is seen in their child they can identify the child with all activities of this type for the remainder of the child's life. An example of such an overgeneralized reaction might be that of tagging a child as a drug addict when it is learned that the child has smoked a bit of marijuana. Such overgeneralizations do have their effect on the child. They usually promote the kind of behavior by the child that is being predicted in the generalization. The tendency to take the occasion of some particular undesirable behavior to generalize that the child is all bad must be avoided. The tendency to predict a big hunk of a child's future based on a small item in the present must likewise be avoided in parental decision-making.

Parents also need to be careful to avoid guilt by association in their decision-making processes. A child can associate with children who partake in undesirable activities without necessarily engaging in the undesirable activities in question. In fact, in the public schools, children often interact with other children in a way that some parents may consider undesirable. Yet, this is no reason to assign the undesirable habits of a few children to the whole student body. In many cases, the child has no choice but to interact with these so-called undesirable children while in the school setting.

Parents Don't Need All the Answers

Parents do not have to have all the answers to all their children's problems. If parents would only stop and realize this, it would come as a great relief to many of them. Children can and do maintain their respect for a parent who says, "I don't know the answer. You might check with so and so. Maybe they can help you. They have had more experience in that area than I have had. Let me know what you find out about it." If children develop an idealized picture of their parents as being all-knowing, they are in for a letdown when that picture becomes marred in later life. They will surely learn that their parents are not gods and that their parents indeed have their own fallibilities.

Children have a reduced chance of knowing something—particularly something that their parents do not know—if their parents are always all-knowing. A child's self-image is boosted several notches when he can tell a parent something new that the parent does not already know. For a child to know more in some area than his or her parents know is perfectly acceptable to the child and should be just as acceptable to the parents. This reversed situation also can give parents an opportunity to take pride justifiably in their offspring's knowledge. Knowledge possessed by children but not by their parents enhances the children and gives then a good vantage point from which they can take part in the decision-making process. It gives children a needed opportunity to practice a degree of independence.

An occasion may arise when it is desirable to ask your children to try to put themselves in your position as a parent just long enough to give you advice about some difficult problem being encountered. The problem may or may not involve the children. A sincere request for advice from children will, in most cases, be met with a sincere, thoughtful reply from a child. There will be times when children come up with unexpected, innovative, and viable alternatives for their parents. To a greater extent than is needed, parents feel they must solve their children's problems and help them make all decisions. It is a refreshing change for everyone to reverse the roles and allow the children to help solve some of their parents' problems. Nothing builds the self-esteem of children more than having their parents seek their advice—unless possibly it is to see their parents actually follow their advice.

Must Parental Decisions Be Unanimous?

Parents are not obligated to always agree completely with each other on matters affecting their children. Disagreements arising from parental decision making can be experienced without one parent trying to undo what the other parent has done as happened in the following case:

> Cynthia and James had four children between the ages of six and eleven. The father's work required him to be away most nights. James and Cynthia also operated a small camera shop, which took all of James' spare time and kept Cynthia away from home five days a week. James fairly much left the child-rearing up to Cynthia, who constantly felt caught in a bind between the chores of motherhood and the chores of the camera store. James did not seem to feel much responsibility to enjoy recreational activities together with his children, but Cynthia felt an obligation and an ever-present sense of guilt for not spending still more time with the children.

Early one Sunday afternoon, the children asked if they could go fishing in a small pond nearby. James told the children that they could not go as he left the house for the camera store. The children, of course, went to work on their mother just as soon as their father had left the house. Cynthia was deluged with begging and pleading behavior from the children. The children began to occupy her time almost constantly with their insistence. The clincher came when seven-year-old Jimmy told his mother, "But Mommy, you are the boss around here. Daddy is gone now. You always decide on what to do at our house." Cynthia gave in and let them go fishing—but not without first issuing a stern warning not to let their father know anything about it so that everyone could stay out of trouble.

This parental disagreement over allowing the children to go fishing could probably have been resolved had both parents remained engaged in the decision-making process a little longer. And to secretly override the father's decision after mother and children had seemingly agreed to comply is inappropriate and helps to establish the father as Mr. Bad Guy in the eyes of his children. Cynthia's reinforcement of the children's ploy to pit one parent against the other only serves to teach the children to apply similar deceptive tactics when they become adults. They begin to believe they can get what they want from other adults when a first adult does not comply, a behavior that is apt to backfire in adult life when their associates learn of their manipulative schemes.

Insist That Children Make Their Own Tough Decisions

Occasionally, it becomes easier for teen-agers to let their parents say no for them than to speak out for themselves. This tactic was sometimes practiced by Sonya and Tonya, fourteen-year-old identical twins. If several members of their gang were at the twins' house, it was common for their parents to be approached by the twins and their friends with a request to go somewhere together. The twins usually pleaded a good case, but there were times when their parents declined permission. In more than one instance, when the twins stayed behind as their friends left the house, there were dual sighs of relief that their parents had said no. In front of their friends, the girls had verbalized a desire to go along and be part of the "gang," but they were actually hoping their parents would not allow them to go. In these instances, they either did not want to go to the place in question or did not want to go with the particular group involved.

I would have said yes a few times when I detected their false intentions in front of friends if I had been their parents. This would serve to encourage them to make and stick by their own decisions even when the decisions obviously would not be popular with their peers. When their friends were not around, the opportunity could be taken to encourage the twins to do their own thinking and to develop enough courage to stand behind that thinking in the face of opposition from friends. Doing their own thinking could understandably be threatening if Sonya and Tonya thought it might cost them some friends. Yet, children with a sufficient self-image can usually bounce back and maintain or reestablish damaged friendships that are important to them.

7
Who Is Responsible?

A father and mother leave home each morning to work at jobs for which they are paid. Their children do no work; nevertheless, they are paid. In most homes, children are paid by way of an allowance. Even in nonallowance homes, children enjoy rewards just the same—rewards that only the parents' labor has earned. This scene describes too many homes in the United States today. But the situation does not have to exist, and where it does, it can be altered.

Children Need Responsibility

Work is a large part of a broader concept, responsibility. It is a major responsibility with which children need to become acquainted.

Children of all ages need responsibility in some form. Responsibility represents a broad area of opportunity in which parents can prepare children for their teen years. Young people too often find themselves in crisis situations when the suddenly imposed responsibilities of higher education, career planning, and the need for increased social interaction occur. If parents have gradually increased the number and complexity of responsibilities for their children, the responsibility for making educational, career and marital choices will simply be more of the same for them. These situations will not be strange new experiences for the young adult who has been trained to accept responsibility; rather, they can be regarded as opportunities to use already learned competencies. Like adults, children attain contentment as they become aware of their abilities to influence their environment in a positive manner.

Responsibility Promotes Belonging

Children as young as two years should and can be given responsibility around the home so they can readily perceive where they fit into the maintenance of the family. When important responsibilities are distributed among all family members, each has a part in helping the family to function as a discrete social entity. Each child needs to experience the satisfaction of contributing—the joy of producing—even if it involves producing something as simple as a washed car or a supply of barbecued hamburgers for dinner.

It is also appropriate for parents to arrange the circumstances in a younger child's environment in a manner that increases the probability of success. Parental assistance to improve the chance of success is particularly useful when a young child undertakes a completely new endeavor. The same applies when children attempt to complete more complex tasks than those to which they have been accustomed. Contrived assured success, however, is harmful. The success must depend on the child's own efforts in persistently addressing a task.

The environment of smaller children can usually be arranged to allow children to do some things for themselves. This is especially true in a child's room, where the selection, size, and placement of furniture can be used to make the child more self-sufficient. Doing things for themselves in turn allows children to develop self-reliance and self-esteem at an early age. Preschool children can do much of the cleaning in and around their rooms. They enjoy feeling like adults by doing things for themselves. Parents must make participation by the child possible, however, by arranging the physical environment so the child does not have to depend on a parent to accomplish all of his or her objectives.

Age-Appropriate Responsibilities

How does one give responsibility to an eight-year-old? For the five percent or so of American farm families, there is no particular problem in looking for responsibilities to assign children. There may be more jobs to go around than there are family members to which to assign them. But what about the other ninety-five percent—the children who live in cities and suburbs and who have never come closer to a cow than the milk they put on their cereal? There are, in fact, numerous tasks in which modern-day urban youths can participate. A creative parent can undoubtedly add more activities to the following list of 101 responsibilities, arranged in ascending order from earliest age of assignment:

The two-year-old can:
1. Put napkins on table for meals
2. Hold dustpan for parent
3. Dry hands and face after being washed
4. Hang coat on hook placed at child's height
5. Bring in newspaper from porch
6. Feed self with fork and spoon
7. Put on socks
8. Pick up and put away toys

The three-year-old can:
9. Call family members to table at mealtime
10. Place coat on hanger
11. Zip own clothing
12. Answer telephone
13. Wash arms and legs in tub
14. Put away own clothes in drawers
15. Brush teeth
16. Conserve food at meals (not wasteful)
17. Place dirty clothes in hamper
18. Comb and brush hair

The four-year-old can:
19. Bath self completely except for shampoo
20. Dress self completely
21. Clean up spills
22. Button clothing
23. Clear place at table after meals
24. Serve self at table
25. Choose clothing to wear from drawers
26. Clean own bedroom
27. Feed pets

The five-year-old can:
28. Conserve electricity and water
29. Tie shoes
30. Clean pet area
31. Be punctual for school and other appointments
32. Shampoo own hair
33. Set table
34. Prepare own cold cereal
35. Walk to school if within two blocks
36. Buckle seat belt in car

The six-year-old can:

37. Complete music or dance practice independently
38. Clean weeds from garden
39. Do homework (school)
40. Manage an allowance
41. Set own alarm clock
42. Carry out trash
43. Make beds
44. Set table

The seven-year-old can:

45. Clean off kitchen countertops
46. Dust furniture, shelves, and window sills
47. Change bed linens
48. Sort incoming family mail
49. Sweep floors
50. Wash and dry dishes
51. Water flowers and plants
52. Prepare simple dishes for meals
53. Write letters to friends and grandparents

The eight-year-old can:

54. Attend athletic practice
55. Cut coupons from advertisements
56. Sow vegetables in garden
57. Harvest vegetables and fruit from garden
58. Plant and tend flowers
59. Rake leaves from lawn
60. Put away laundry
61. Take accurate written phone messages

The nine-year-old can:

62. Buy gifts for others using own money
63. Purchase needed school supplies
64. Put away groceries
65. Repair broken games, lamps, simple items
66. Vacuum house
67. Wash windows inside

The ten-year-old can:

68. Balance family checkbook
69. Barbecue and grill meat
70. Clean bathroom fixtures
71. Iron clothes
72. Open and close windows as weather changes
73. Load dishwasher
74. Prepare complete meal for family

The eleven-year-old can:

75. Mend clothing
76. Paint house and fences
77. Do lawn mower maintenance
78. Mop floors
79. Mow lawn
80. Wash car

The twelve-year-old can:

81. Shop for groceries
82. Babysit
83. Make clothing
84. Purchase cosmetic and health aids
85. Purchase (choose) own clothes
86. Renew magazine subscriptions
87. Wash and dry clothes

The thirteen-year-old can:

88. Change furnace filter
89. Plan family food budget
90. Scan grocery advertisements for needed specials
91. Perform routine auto maintenance

The fourteen-year-old can:

92. Repair lawn mower
93. Manage a checking account
94. Manage a savings account
95. Make own medical and dental appointments

The fifteen-year-old can:

96. Arrange furniture
97. Do car repair
98. Put on and take off auto snow tires

The sixteen-year-old can:

99. Drive family car (if allowed by law)
100. Verify and pay bills (by mail or with car)
101. Secure after-school, weekend, and summer jobs

Simple, repetitive tasks appear at the earlier ages on the list. More complex tasks, requiring multiple steps, advanced reasoning, and decision-making skills, begin to appear in the teen-aged years. As a child of nine, for instance, learns to vacuum the house, the teacher, usually a parent, will probably begin by demonstrating the sequential steps involved. When the basics are learned and can be completed unassisted, parents need to be alert for and receptive to changes that the child wishes to introduce in the approach used to accomplish a task. As a child becomes older, more intricate house cleaning responsibilities can be assigned. Perhaps a complete clean house-maintenance contract can be negotiated with the child by age twelve.

The responsibility list for the two-year-old is nearly three times as long as that for the sixteen-year-old. More items are listed for younger children for two reasons: (1) parents can more readily think of responsibilities on their own for high school-aged children than they can for a toddler, and (2) children are capable of learning tasks at a much earlier age than most parents give them credit for. When the earliest age of responsibility assignment is listed, it causes more tasks to be itemized at earlier ages than would be expected.

A number of the tasks in the preceding list can be more quickly completed by an accomplished parent than by a youngster. However, it is infinitely better to take the more difficult route of teaching children to do tasks as soon as they are developmentally capable of acquiring the needed skills. Rest assured that children will make mistakes; however, the very same mistakes may be made a year or more later if the necessary skill teaching is delayed. If learning is delayed until adulthood, the individual is still likely to make some of the same mistakes. It is desirable to let children make some of their mistakes, which results in learning some valuable lessons, while they are still children; in this way, they get a portion of their mistakes behind them. As an adult, mistakes tend to become more costly; also, there is often no parent available to play a supportive role or offer corrective suggestions to the adult. Assuming increasing responsibility, including responsibility for one's mistakes, is part of every individual's learning process and must be accumulated progressively over a lifetime.

In *Parents and Teen-agers: Getting Through to Each Other,* Margaret Albrecht makes the following statement, "Learning who one is not is indispensable to moving closer to who one is. Perhaps most important, the failures teach that one can fail and—whether bounding or climbing a bit stiffly—not only survive but climb farther, or at least pick a different side of the mountain." Children need a chance to fail. Everyone needs a chance to fail, for where there is no chance to fail, there is no challenge, no progressive undertaking accomplished, no responsibility met. And when temporary failure occurs after children have assumed responsibility—what then? This is no time for blaming, judging, cautious reminders, and statements equivalent to "I told you so." Rather, this is the time for parental support, but only to the extent accepted by the child. Overnurturing in the form of excessive attention is not desirable because this kissing-the-hurt behavior tends to reinforce failure by giving it a payoff.

Allowance or Wages Earned

Should children be paid for completing tasks around the house? Perhaps. The question of giving children money can be satisfactorily approached in several ways. Just as adults are paid for the work they do at jobs away from home, children see their being paid for the jobs they do at home as a logical extension of the concept of wages paid for services provided. One approach is for parents to pay children for the work they do. Still, payment does not have to become a habit. Habitual payment for every task performed can cause children to look for financial gain each time they contribute in even the smallest way to any worthwhile cause.

Much flexibility can be built into the parents' policy of paying children for the work they do. The extremes to be avoided are: (1) using children to do a considerable amount of work with no compensation whatsoever and (2) overcompensation in the form of paying children for any and every constructive thing they do around the house. Children can also be overcompensated by paying them much more than their services are worth. This can lead to inflated opinions about the worth of their contributions. Fair market value should be the guiding factor in deciding how much to pay children.

At present, allowances for children are fairly widespread in the United States. Although allowances may work in some circumstances, the concept of regularly giving money to children with no contingencies has more negative than positive attributes. The major negative attribute of a guaranteed allowance is the danger of instilling a something-for-nothing attitude that cannot be maintained for the duration of the child's life.

If an allowance is to be paid, the contingency allowance probably works best. For younger children under the age of twelve, an allowance is best paid daily. Paying the allowance at the same time each day, preferably just before bedtime, is desirable. The allowance is paid only if certain predetermined responsibilities of the day have been satisfactorily completed. If the responsibilities have been satisfied according to pre-established standards, a friendly exchange of money takes place; however, if one or more responsibilities have not been satisfied, a friendly non-exchange takes place. In this instance the only exchange on the part of the parent is a non-accusatory matter-of-fact statement informing the child that particular responsibilities were not satisfactorily completed. It is not a time to haggle over details of the allowance contingencies, and it is not a time to be drawn into parent-child arguments. It is also not a time to negotiate what can be done to make up for the unassumed responsibility, and it is not a time to negotiate an allowance advance. Tomorrow there will be a totally new opportunity to receive another day's allowance. As for today's allowance, the child is the one who must adjust for the missing money; the child is the one who experiences the inconvenience of responsibilities not met.

Must All Work Be Distasteful?

Home tasks, responsibilities, or work, if you prefer, can often be presented in a manner that is not distasteful to children. When children are treated as a valuable part of the family in non-work situations, they are more inclined to feel like part of the family in work situations. They are less resentful of assigned family tasks when the work represents simply one more example of a family activity in which they can participate and have a voice.

Assigning work as punishment is a sure way to teach children to dislike work. Children try to avoid work assigned as punishment. Punishment in the form of work teaches children that work is a curse instead of a blessing—an arbitrarily assigned unpleasantry instead of a creative growth opportunity.

Many children register initial complaints about tasks that are assigned to them. Quite often, though, after the work has been begun and they see fellow family members contributing to the overall effort, one hears singing, whistling, and humming above the roar of the vacuum or the putt-putt of the rotary tiller. The fruits of labor are enjoyed by children and adults alike as they see their progress toward a recognized goal which they understand. We should not be surprised to learn that our children are actually pleased on certain occasions when they are asked to contribute their efforts toward family goal attainment.

If, moreover, children work to the point of being tired, parents need not feel guilty. Little danger of injury to health results from vigorous physical or mental work. It is in such a state of tiredness that children as well as adults learn to appreciate the meaning of rest. Rest is a garnishment to be savored only by the working person as Plutarch recognized when he said, "Rest is the sweet sauce of labor."

A Pitfall in Work Assignment

In a home with two or more children, tasks are too often assigned to the child who is most willing, cooperative, and skilled at a job. This results in an unfair burden on the more willing child while the behavior of the resisting, less-skilled child is reinforced by the child's not having to accept the responsibility for the assigned task. A resisting child may even learn to argue or to only half do tasks by feigning incompetence. This behavior is reinforced when the child is overlooked when there is work to do on future occasions. Reinforcement for resistance and incompetence also occurs when adults intervene and assist or eventually complete the task themselves.

But, the easier approach is not the best. Take time to instruct an unskilled or resisting child in the correct manner in which to complete a task. Provide an ample opportunity for the child to ask questions and clear up uncertainties. The parent should also remain available to answer further questions and to check progress after the task has been started. Parents can definitely avoid the unfortunate circumstance of teaching their children to be quitters or whiners by not allowing them to shirk responsibility with poor-little-me behavior.

The Broader Concept of Responsibility

In his book, *This Is Earl Nightengale,* Nightengale speaks of a "consciousness of competence" that allows an individual to relax and excel without excessive straining or forcing. When chidren are taught responsibilities in a variety of areas, their knowledge and skill increases, and thus, they begin to acquire an awareness of their own competence.

Work activities and related tasks represent only one type of responsibility that children can handle. They can be taught to assume responsibility for their own grooming, health, and safety. Children can also assume responsibility for maintaining satisfactory interpersonal relationships with others—family members, friends, fellow students, and teachers. In the area of interpersonal relationships, parents need to step aside at times and allow their children to get themselves out of tense situations—situations generated by the children in their dealings with others.

Parents need to learn to trust their children's abilities to solve their own problems. Children have a great variety of abilities that often remain latent until adulthood. These budding potentials could develop sooner but only under conditions of minimal parental intervention.

Assuming the Full Scope of Responsibility

Beth's family was alarmed when they learnea that she had a kidney disease that would require three months of hospitalization.

Beth was married and had five children ranging in age from a high-school student to a child who had just come out of diapers. After the initial shock, reverberations continued and even intensified regarding the welfare of the children who would soon be motherless for so long.

Yet, the home situation that developed when Beth entered the hospital proved that any expectations of disaster were false. With guidance from their father, the older children took over the management of the home. They taught and assigned tasks to the younger children as their ages permitted. The smaller children knew that their older siblings were doing their part and were trying to assign responsibility fairly. This, plus the fact that they could clearly see the necessity for organized togetherness, encouraged them to be cooperative and receptive to work assignments. All the children could see where they fit into the family picture.

The older children rose to the occasion and assumed their responsibility with surprising rapidity. Sixteen-year-old George learned to plan meals and do the food shopping. Thirteen-year-old Mary played an auxiliary role in the meal planning and shopping, but her primary task was the weekly laundry. David, who had just turned eleven, diligently cleared the table after meals and washed the dishes. Mark, who was six and would start school next year, felt a need to do his part. His home assignments were things such as feeding the dog, drying pots and pans, and taking clothes from the hamper to the laundry room. He also became an expert at putting away groceries. Tonya, at two and a half, made limited contributions to the overall welfare of the entire family, and she did learn to brush her teeth without being reminded. She became self-sufficient beyond anyone's imagination as she dressed herself, fed herself, and used the toilet without requiring the attention of any other family member.

Necessity forced these children to work together like the parts of a well-oiled machine. At first, there were mistakes. There were several inconsequential accidents. There was less efficiency than their mother displayed when she was at home.

Beth's surgery and treatments were successful, and her hospitalization lasted only two months instead of the expected three. The favorable reports that were passed to her daily by her husband and friends about her family undoubtedly contributed to her recovery. While continuing to recover at home, Beth was able to see her children in action. She was reassured to find that the cooking of her two oldest surpassed the cooking to which she had grown accustomed at the hospital.

This story could be reenacted in most any home in America if it became absolutely necessary for the children to assume the responsibility of managing the house. The message in this story for all parents is the importance of beginning to allow children to assume responsibility and do productive work now—before an emergency makes it mandatory.

Assuming Responsibility for Self

An example of children assuming responsibility for part of their world is shown in the use of an alarm clock. Why should a mother always wake her children and then often reawaken them and nag them to get them up in time for breakfast and school? Even first-grade children are able to set alarm clocks and get themselves out of bed and dressed for school without parental help. If one child should procrastinate and get up so late that the school bus is missed, it is that child's responsibility to come up with a means of transportation to school or possibly to miss a day of school.

Unthinkable? Missing a day of school probably sounds like an awful consequence just for getting up too late to catch a school bus, and one might at first be inclined to think that children might learn to get up late deliberately so they would miss the bus and therefore avoid a day of school. Not so, unless the child is a cynical, confirmed school-hater of high school age. Our twelve-year-old found himself with a missed bus situation after repeatedly getting up at the last possible moment on several consecutive mornings. On a morning when the bus came a full sixty seconds early, a crisis point had been reached. He stood watching the smoke from the exhaust as the bus rounded the corner.

He had been informed earlier that he was expected to get moving each morning in time to catch the assigned school bus. Otherwise he could anticipate the consequences that would involve finding his own transportation or missing a day of school. He prefered the alternative of missing a day of school to that of securing his own transportation. Perhaps he really wanted to test his parents' policy to see if he would actually be allowed to miss a full day of school. He spent the day alone at home. The next morning his alarm sounded a full ten minutes before anyone else's alarm. The remainder of the school year was completed without a single missed bus and without another warning word being spoken.

Taking Responsibility for Relations with Peers

As children assume responsibility for themselves, they can also be expected to assume responsibility for selecting their friends. Parental selection of and interaction with their own peers serves as a model for children to follow as they choose their peers. The most useful way for parents to participate in their children's friend-selection process is via the home living arrangement. Hopefully, an adequate supply of age-appropriate peers are available for friendship formation in the neighborhood. If parents should feel strong concern about their children's choice of friends, they can best deal with this by explicitly communicating it to the child as opposed to using implicit derogatory remarks. If parents choose to verbalize their concern, they will need to be careful to exercise their listening skills when their children talk about their friends.

Siblings commonly initiate rivalries and have arguments and fights among themselves. It is almost as common to see one child run to a parent demanding punishment for a brother or sister for some unprovoked attack. The justice demanded usually takes the form of "Make Johnny give my ball back," or "Punish Mary for the awful thing she did to me."

Parents too often do enter such arenas of conflict and set themselves up as judges or referees for every complaint related to sibling interaction. Parents would do better suddenly to become hard of hearing in these situations. Temporarily leaving the scene is also a useful way for parents to avoid hearing complaints and becoming involved as a peacemaker. Within the framework of saving smaller children from severe physical blows from larger children, a parent's response should be that the rivalry is between the children and that they are expected to work out differences among themselves. This gives the children the responsibility of dealing with their own interpersonal relationships. It also prevents children from becoming adults who will continue to turn authority figures to set everything right each time another adult perpetrates an alleged injustice.

It is certainly difficult to tell a young child to "settle the problem yourself" when an older and larger sibling is involved. But only if the health or safety of the younger child is seriously threatened should a parent intervene. It is better to speak to the older child at a later time so the younger child will not be inadvertently reinforced for running to the parents. Neither child should learn to associate solutions to inter-personal problems with reporting to either parent.

Property Rights Responsibility

Children can best learn responsibility for property rights by having property of their own. Earlier in this chapter, the different options available to parents to help their children acquire money that could be used to obtain their own property were described. In addition to the many ways children can earn money at home, older children can earn money in their neighborhoods from after-school, weekend, and summer jobs. Parents should exercise wide latitude in allowing children to use their money as they wish to further their individual interests.

A concerned father who stayed awake nights worrying about his son's newfound independence related the following story to me.

> His son, Eddie, did not bother to ask his parents if he could walk to a lake a mile away to go fishing. With rod and reel and tackle box in hand, he simply announced he was going fishing and would be back in a few hours. His mother gave his father a penetrating look as if to say, "He is your son." Father was about to admonish his son for not asking for permission when he remembered what had been discussed in an earlier therapy session about withdrawing from his tendency toward overcontrol. He remembered the discussion about allowing his son to display some independence to see if the boy could handle it in a responsible manner. So the father said, "OK. Thanks for telling us where you will be. I'll help you clean your catch if you need me."
>
> When Eddie returned, later than expected, he did not have a string of fish to display, but he did have a tale to tell. When asked if he had gotten many bites, he said that he had not had much time for fishing. It seems he had left some extra lures in a paper bag along the lake bank as he cast his favorite lure from some undergrowth a few hundred yards away. When he returned, he noted that two plugs and three bass flies were missing from the bag. As he scratched his head in puzzlement, two boys—casual acquaintances—appeared with rods and reels tipped with lures just like those missing from Eddie's bag. Eddie instantly recognized his missing lures and confronted the boys demanding his lures back. He strongly suspected they also had taken his missing flies and he demanded his flies back as well. The boys denied any knowledge of the lures, but Eddie knew better.
>
> He thought he knew where one of the boys lived, and he went to the house and asked to see the boy's parents. A gruff father came to the door, but Eddie was not intimidated as he related his story of the missing lures. Eddie also asked and was told where the other boy lived. He immediately went to that house and again told his story to the parents there. The parents did listen to him and agreed that the boy he described was their son. Eddie's story was apparently believable to both sets of parents, because they began to search the neighborhood for their sons.
>
> At this point Eddie had told no one else, not even his parents, and had not contacted or threatened to contact the police. When the fathers of both boys found their sons, the boys initially denied that they had taken Eddie's lures. But the stern admonitions of each father and the supplying of accurate descriptions of the still missing lures by Eddie caused the boys to

give way to their fathers' interrogations. The boys led their fathers and Eddie to a clump of bushes near the lake where they had hidden the missing flies and plugs. Eddie was relieved and grateful to have his lures back. He thanked each father and headed home.

Had either of Eddie's parents known of his involvement in this incident, their anxiety levels would have risen. When presented with a *fait accompli*, Eddie's father realized that his son had handled the theft incident beautifully. He had depended on his own limited knowledge of the incident and his persistence to recover his property. He had not depended on his mother or father or the police to bail him out. Eddie had shown that he could respond appropriately to responsibility. He was genuinely ready to accept more independence from his parents. Eddie's newly found self-reliance caused his parents to feel a little less needed, which was threatening to them but none-the-less represented progress for all the family.

Assuming Parental Responsibility

Perhaps parents reading this book can remember times when they asked one parent for permission to do something and were told to ask the other parent. There is a good chance that the other parent, when approached, said, "Well, you'd better check with your mother (father)." This familiar parental ploy is merely a dodge. Parents must on occasion accept the responsibility for making difficult decisions that affect their children. It is easy to pass on responsibility to one's spouse when faced with a difficult decision that could lead to negative consequences either way the decision is made. If a difficult decision is passed on to a spouse, one can then lay any blame for a wrong decision at his or her feet. This is often the unconscious motive behind "Go ask your mother (father)" statements. Forcing someone else to make a decision that is one's own problem is first-order responsibility shunning. Blaming another person for a less-than-desirable outcome is even more inappropriate.

When one parent feels inadequate to handle a decision, it is time for a parent conference, in which a joint decision can be reached. If, however, one parent is definitely in a better position to make a particular decision, it is up to that parent to go with the child to the other parent. The parent who feels less competent to make the decision should frankly relate this to his or her spouse. The decision of the spouse should then be accepted as the most expedient course of action and should not be questioned after the fact. This type of parental process and support represents the assumption of parental responsibility and models it in an appropriate manner for children.

8
Accentuate the Positive

Keeping lists of another's faults (alleged or otherwise) rarely helps any relationship and often hinders it. The following story involves one mother who did keep score as her daughter failed more and more to live up to her extraordinary expectations for her.

Jerrie seemed to be a calm enough fourteen-year-old girl when her father and mother brought her to the clinic for alleged behavioral problems. She appeared intelligent and alert and was responsive to questions and to the environment in general. Jerrie's mother was exceptionally verbose and precise in describing Jerrie's misdeeds, which she said had originated in kindergarten.

The secret of the mother's terrific memory was revealed on the second visit. While Jerrie waited in a private counseling room, her mother showed me a standard size black school notebook. It contained a complete biography of Jerrie from the time she was three up until the very day of the visit. The notebook should have had a big minus on its front, because ninety-five percent of the entries were negative statements about Jerrie. The black book, in fact, represented the ultimate in negativism. It started by telling of Jerrie's youthful desire to see her older brother naked, included a broken window when she was eight, and concluded with the finding of cigarette wrapping papers in Jerrie's purse, papers that, according to Jerrie's mother, were obviously used to roll marijuana cigarettes. The seventy-eight page biography told of the shortcomings, failures, and unfulfilled parental expectations of a young girl. The mother said, "Look at all the despicable things she has done to us after all we have done for her."

Entries in the notebook had been carefully dated, and each was numbered for ready reference. So thorough was the woman at collecting evidence that she would have made an excellent district attorney.

The mother's detective work was unnecessary and rather than alleviating the problem had only aggravated it. After a few more sessions, Jerrie's mother was encouraged to destroy the notebook. We had a book burning ceremony, at which time Jerrie's mother agreed also to purge her thinking of all the misdeeds she had observed in her daughter. An immediate improvement in the mother's mental health was evident.

So far, it would seem that the onus for behavioral change is totally on the mother, leaving the daughter free to continue her inappropriate behavior. Yet, at the book burning session, Jerrie volunteered to do her part to insure that no one ever again had cause to start another black book about her. Parents must learn to forgive their children—to let go of a negative past—just as surely as they need to accept the fact they may need forgiveness from their children at some point.

The Other Black Book: Religion Out of Context

It is fairly common for zealously religious parents with a child in trouble to quote the ages-old standby, "Spare the rod and spoil the child." Some of these parents quote specific verses from the Bible such as Proverbs 23:13—"Do not withhold discipline from a child"—or Exodus 21:14—"Honor your father and mother...," which is one of the Ten Commandments. Unfortunately, few parents are familiar with Ephesians 6:4, which states, "Fathers, do not provoke your children to anger."

The few parents who do go all out to impose their strict religious beliefs onto children run amuck when the parenting and religious training they provide takes the form of an extreme need to be in control. This was the situation with Al, a fifteen-year-old high school sophomore who could not wait until he was sixteen so he could start driving.

> One Sunday afternoon Al's parents were returning home from a church meeting with friends. As they neared home, they saw Al whizzing their second car into the driveway, battered fender and all. How could this be? There were only two sets of keys, and each parent had a set. Al was only fifteen; he did not even know how to drive the car.
>
> Al was in the house as they pulled into the driveway. When they finally caught up with Al, he was in his room at his desk, algebra book in hand. "What? Why all the hassle? Had someone

taken the car out of the driveway?" he asked. Initially, he admitted to nothing and even did a fine job of feigning surprise. It took Al, Senior, and his wife less than five minutes to convince Al that they had seen him enter the driveway in their car as they approached from the other end of the block. Since the truth was overwhelming at this point, Al started to talk. He had had his own ignition key made from mother's key down at the hardware store a few weeks earlier. Al felt it was the only alternative he had left. He had passed driver training at school. He was old enough for a driving permit, but his father had said no. According to Al, father had made him feel guilty for even asking. His father had a different perspective. According to him, the church was only two blocks away, within walking distance for Al. His mother agreed, Al did not need to be going anyplace else where he could only "get into trouble." His parents felt betrayed: Why had Al deceived them in this way?

Why? To this psychologist, this word *why*, and its equivalents signify the height of parental negativism. The explicit message in a why statement is, "What were your motives?" It does not help parents to ask children their motives. What happens after the word *why* is directed to a child following an event evoking parental disapproval? The possible situations surrounding parental whys can be placed in one of three categories.

Category 1: The child does not know why. This category probably covers over half of all parental whys. The younger the child, the higher the percentage of parental whys in category one. Consciously, the child is actually unaware of why he or she has done something and is telling the truth when he or she says, "I don't know why." Further insistence on a reason by parents only forces a child to create some rationale to try to satisfy the inquisitors.

Category 2: The child knows why but lies about it. When children are aware of why they did something that is construed negatively by others, they are inclined to take what looks like the easiest way out. This misrepresentation can take two forms: (1) claiming not to know why and (2) making up a diversionary story. Children will lie when the risk of telling the truth seems too great and the anticipated negative consequences in store for them seem too certain. More than a few parents force their children to learn to lie when they insist on knowing the child's reasons.

Category 3: The child knows why and tells the truth. Great! The parents think they are getting somewhere now. But where? What will they do with the truth? How do they use the child's motives to improve the situation? The psychologist, the child psychiatrist, the family counselor—these professionals are best equipped to discern a child's true motives and prescribe treatment based partially on these motives. As a rule, parents are ineffectual in establishing the true motives of a resisting child, and, like the dog who finally caught the car it had been chasing, most parents do not know what to do with the facts when they get them.

Al stuck to his Category 1 explanation and refused to tell why he had taken an illegal jaunt in the family car. He was genuinely unaware of his own motivation for this action. If his unconscious mind could talk, however, it would have said something such as, "I am tired of my parents telling me everything I can and can't do—everything a good boy should and shouldn't do. I am frustrated at not being allowed to go anywhere except to church. I have absorbed the humiliation of putdown after putdown as I've tried to gain some independence from my overwatchful, distrusting parents. The humiliations I've absorbed have built up pressure inside me, and I must let off some steam from time to time. When I do something such as taking their car for an unauthorized drive, I get back at them for their excessive control. And that dent I put in their precious fender—that is just partial repayment for the many times they have dented my day-to-day plans. It seems like the only time I ever had control over anything was when I roared off in the family car. I controlled the car and it responded instantly—something I had never experienced before. There is no way I could ever hope to please them. I used to try, but I was never able to measure up to their rigid standards, so I've quit trying. What's the use? No matter what I did, it wouldn't be good enough."

It took this unfortunate precipitating event to persuade Al's parents to realize that their methods—moralizing, controlling, indoctrinating, and restricting—were not working. In this case religion had served as a crutch to allow Al's parents to accentuate the negative at the expense of not even looking for the positive. It took two months of weekly family therapy before Al began to get in touch with his feelings and to open up. He had been taught that parents are always right because they were parents. His upbringing had taught him to never disagree with his parents, a frame of mind that certainly left no place for anger. After another two months of treatment Al was finally able to tell himself and his parents the essence of this message.

Negative Turned Positive: Religion in Context

Al's parents eventually got in touch with what happens when one provokes one's children to anger, and then, for the first time, they began to use their religion as a parenting asset instead of detriment. They learned to trust their son and showed this by their support of his application for a driving permit. A few months later, his father took Al to get his driver's license on his sixteenth birthday. The family had more work to do on their interpersonal relationships, but they had certainly come a long way as Al drove the car into the driveway that day. His mother, and eventually his father, began to realize that their boy could get into as much trouble right around home as he could across town at some nonchurch function, so Al was now given some long overdue breathing room.

Parents do not have to put their Bibles away to rear children, but they should certainly be alert to the parental propensity to use this black book as a crutch in supporting unhealthy, one-sided relations with children. Caution is also needed so parents will not use the Bible as a club over their children's heads to point out every perceived negative behavior. Religion should and definitely can be a parenting asset when it is used to accentuate the positive, ignore much of the negative, and forgive the rest.

The Test of Importance

When debating whether or not to establish a new guideline or rule for children, consider whether a rule or guideline is even needed. Does it pass the importance test? First, consider what would likely happen if the rule were not made. Perhaps the expected results would be about the same with or without any input from the parents in the form of a new rule. If a new parental rule is not likely to have a significant beneficial effect on a child's behavior, it fails the test of importance and is not needed; the rule should be left unsaid.

Even when an issue passes this test, parents still need to avoid generalizing with statements such as, "Now be nice at the party, dear" or "You be careful when you ride your bike over to Jimmy's house." Just what does it mean to be nice at a party, and what is necessary to "be careful" while biking to a friend's house? If there are specific behaviors that are important for a child to do at a party, then these particular behaviors should be itemized in sufficient detail to allow the child to know exactly what is expected. If there are important behaviors that the child is to avoid at the party, mention should be made of them. If they are not worth itemizing explicitly, parents might just as well remain quiet about the whole thing and say something like "Have a good time at the party" or "Eat a piece of cake for me, OK?" Parties are for having fun, but it is difficult to enjoy them when children leave home with a half dozen vague behavioral rules ringing in their ears.

A second consideration regarding rule-making is the parents' ability to enforce a rule. Is it important enough to enforce? If parents cannot assure themselves that a new rule will be complied with, it should never be established. Perhaps natural consequences are such that an unpleasant situation automatically develops whenever the child engages in undesirable behavior. This negates the need for rule-making, and policing by parents. Natural consequences are preferred over artificial or arbitrary parental rules as an effort is made to accentuate positive behavior while eliminating negative behavior.

Communicating an Expectation

If you establish that your children need to be informed of a particular parental expectation, that is, if the expectation passes the importance test, then how will the expectation be communicated? The technique of using snide, implicit remarks with uncalled-for insinuations sandwiched among the explicit portions of a conversation is an outdated maneuver. Parents need to learn to present their expectations in a tentative yet explicit way. This can be done through proposals presented for the child's consideration. The parents' reasoning and the child's reasoning can be examined in an open atmosphere. The children may well develop their own separate proposals or offer counter proposals. When agreement on a proposal cannot be reached, it is time for both parties to start thinking in terms of compromise. Perhaps parents can concede some minor points that the children hold dear while they stand firm in areas they consider essential for the well-being of the children.

If no compromise is forthcoming and parents still strongly feel that their own view is clearly to the children's ultimate advantage, it is time for the parents to state their reasons and expectations in the form of rules. Parents need to accentuate their feelings of positive regard for their children when a concensus is not reached. It is possible to go against a child's wishes without going against the child. Determined parents can like their child while they dislike his or her past behaviors or proposed ideas. Determined parents can state their important limits and rules with an attitude of positive expectation.

False Positives: Praise and When to Use It

It is good policy to reinforce and justifiably praise children for their positive behaviors—even in front of other family members. Each additional family member is one more source of reinforcement for desirable behavior. Giving children deserved verbal reinforcement for their positive behaviors in the presence of others gives them a good name to live up to, which makes it easier to justify the confidence their parents have in them. Puffery and false flattery are not called for in dealing with children any more than they are in dealing with adults. They are nothing more than false positives, and they represent one form of parental insincerity. Such insincerity is readily detected by children who usually have a good idea of the merits of their own behavior and accomplishments. Children may consciously pick up a sense of falseness—a negative connotation—in an adult's indiscriminate praise. Even if children have no conscious awareness of the adult's insincerity, that insincerity may nevertheless be recorded at an unconscious level. Either way, the message is the same: It implies to children that their performance is not good enough in and of itself and must be blown out of proportion and exaggerated before it is worthy of merit.

The "I Told You So" Parent

Children may be allowed to do something their own way if they insist, but only if it does not endanger anyone's safety, destroy property, or infringe on another individual's rights. Should a child's method fail in a case where the property and rights of others have not been affected, nothing particularly need be said about it. Certainly there is no place for a parental "I told you so." Failure to achieve a sought-after goal may be aversive enough to cause the child to abandon or modify an approach. Yet learning derived from experience is called wisdom by some, and in any event it is an effective teacher. When a child's method is successful, he enjoys a sense of accomplishment, and the behaviors that led to the success are automatically accentuated with an increased probability that they will be repeated.

Finding Success in Failure

What many people call failure is often merely a temporary lack of success. In most such failure (temporary lack of success) there is never-the-less the seed of a future success; however, that seed must be located, planted, and nourished in order to produce success from what started out as failure. Children must be taught to seek out the bits of success stowed away in their seeming failures. One hundred percent failure is rare. The primary objective may have been lost, but with careful searching, some fragments of truth may be assembled, some bits of learning acquired. These can be used to attempt to reach the same objective at another time or in another way. Perhaps the truths derived from several failures can be put together and serve to help establish another, more attainable objective. Perhaps the learning can be transferred to assist in formulating and attaining other objectives in totally unrelated areas.

The Negative Approach to Positiveness

Just because parents are in a position to exercise power over their children is certainly no reason for doing so. Parents are older and almost always larger than their children for the first fifteen years. Parents are recognized by society as having responsibility for and authority over their children. This puts each parent at a tactical advantage, but it also appreciably lessens the need to actually use the control and authority. An overwhelming application of power by a parent may bring temporary compliance on a child's part, but it also may bring long-range defiance. Children who are regularly overpowered begin to think of physical size and the power it appears to bring as worthwhile goals. They long for the time when they will be physically large and can get away with the hostile, aggressive behavior they see their parents using on them. And when they achieve physical maturity, it is a safe bet that they will use their size and aggressive anger as a means of exercising power to control others.

Parents sometimes voice the concern that their children will lose respect for them if they do not deal with the children from a position of power—a concern that is ungrounded. If a child loses anything in the absence of parental power, it will be the fear of parents, and this is an excellent thing to lose. Respect is in fact lost when parents capitalize on their greater physical size and authority in the family always to get their way with children.

9
What to Expect of Whom

Occasionally parents are disappointed by their children. The first way a child can disappoint its parents and not live up to their expectations is by being a girl when a boy was desired, or by being a boy when a girl was desired. At this writing, parents cannot control the sex of their children physically; nor should they try to control their child's sex psychologically, although some do. Psychological sex changes involve such things as giving a girl an obvious boy's name or dressing a boy in girl's clothes. Parents-to-be can save themselves some mental anguish by not building up excessive expectations for one sex or the other before birth. At least, they should refrain from this until sex control becomes a reality.

Sex stereotypes are still common in most countries. Such stereotypes are being gradually removed in many locations, so that being a particular sex does not consign an individual strictly to the attitudes and behaviors heretofore associated with that sex. Parents today need to withdraw sufficiently to allow their children to develop their natural interests without the strict limits that society has known.

What Causes Lazy Children?

What causes a lazy child? Do so-called lazy children come from homes where little is expected of them? Yes, some do. But lazy children are also generated in another kind of home, namely one in which the parents have very high expectations of their child. It soon becomes obvious to the child that it is impossible to succeed in this kind of environment, especially if the child's intelligence or native ability is below that of the parents. The child reasons that, since he or she is certain to fail in meeting the parents' high standards, there is nothing to be gained by putting forth any excessive effort. After all, who can accuse a child of failing who really never tried in the first place? Expectations of children should be in proportion to the reality of their ability, their stage of development, and their experience. A good book to be consulted with regard to a child's sensory development is *The Psychological Development of the Child* by Paul H. Mussen.

When parents expect too much of children, it is common to criticize them for not living up to those expectations. This not only causes children to feel inadequate, but also causes them to sometimes become overly critical of themselves. Children can become self-condemning to the point where they set standards so high that their attainment is all but impossible. They begin to feel inadequate, which can bring on the harshest form of criticism, self-criticism. Such children too often become adults who specialize in expecting too much of self and too much of others. They are thereby frequently disappointed when these high expectations are not fulfilled. They feel that people have let them down. Worse still is the devastating feeling that they have let others down by not living up to what they thought others expected of them.

Parental Aspirations

It is not uncommon for parents to saddle their children with their own unfulfilled childhood aspirations. In these situations, the child is encouraged by the parents to want something or to seek a goal to which great worth is attributed by parents who were themselves unable to achieve the goal. Some parents even try to make their children feel guilty if the children do not also express the need that the parents have in mind for them. Unreasonable expectations cause children to go into adulthood not really belonging to themselves. They belong to others, namely, their parents, and they feel guilty when they are not doing what others expect of them.

Ironically, many of these unmet parental aspirations could still be accomplished by the parents, if they would only generate the courage to make the necessary sacrifices. Such parental action would then leave the children free to develop and work toward their own aspirations.

Inconsistency in Teen-Agers

The change from childhood to adulthood is bumpy and uneven with most children. Teen-agers act like adults one day and like children the next. This touch-and-go behavior often manifests itself in a manner similar to that seen by Sylvia's parents.

Sylvia was an active fourteen-year-old who appeared happy and fairly free of life's problems. Therefore, it came as a surprise to her parents one day when she bombarded them with questions about what she might like to do when she finished school. Thoughts of "our little girl is growing up" ran through the parents' minds as they tried to respond in a reasonable manner without appearing too surprised. Her parents seemed a little unknowing and confused as Sylvia discussed some of her thinking with them, because neither her mother nor her father had used any time to plan Sylvia's educational and career goals. This worked fine, because it put Sylvia's parents on her level. Their lack of planning made it easier for her to talk to them without feeling inferior and uninformed. The discussion lasted less than ten minutes, and it failed to settle any definitive questions or to provide an all-encompassing plan for Sylvia. The topics discussed remained ambiguous and unsettling to all concerned. The fact that no concrete conclusions were drawn did not make the shocked and dazed parents feel at all well, but this did not bother Sylvia. In fact, Sylvia felt better, because she had verbalized some of her thinking. She had "tried it on for size" and had taken the opportunity to hear how some of her thinking sounded when spoken to someone. Her parents were not evaluative of her thinking, because they did not have time to formulate their own opinions on the matter. This proved to be a fortunate point, because it left the door open for further discussions at a later time.

Sylvia's parents were ready to continue the discussion the next afternoon when she arrived home from school. They had put much thought into the matter since the first career-planning session the previous day. Sylvia, however, dashed in and out of the kitchen with a quick hi and was next seen two houses down the street playing kickball with ten and eleven-year-old children in the neighborhood.

Sylvia's parents' initial feeling of surprise turned to anger as they thought of all the input they had made into the problem during the previous twenty-four hours. They thought of all the difficult decisions they had made for her. Then they paused, looked at each other, and smiled as they simultaneously felt relieved to realize that their daughter had not yet grown up after all. Parents of early adolescents can expect to see this erratic adult-child behavior from their teen-aged children. As children approach late adolescence, less of the childlike behavior will be sprinkled in a matrix of largely adultlike behavior.

Parents can expect their teen-aged children to be arrogantly independent one day and uninformed and indecisive the next. It serves no useful purpose to make a big point of telling children that some of their behavior is infantile, that they should grow up. Nothing is accomplished by telling a fourteen-year-old boy that he should not be too scared to stand up in front of his class and present a biology report. He would not have been told that at age seven; neither does he need to be told to be unafraid at age fourteen, an age at which a little of the seven-year-old boy still resides in him.

Effective parents learn not to expect adult behavior from their teen-agers all the time. We expect adult behavior from adults, but we do not get it all of the time either. The ranks of adults who sometimes function like children is astounding, so why should we expect teen-agers to behave more adultlike than adults? Thomas A. Harris, author of *I'm OK, You're OK*, tells of many of these childlike behaviors that are seen every day in our adult associates; many apply to teen-agers.

A fourteen-year-old girl will not feel any more mature after carelessly throwing pizza dough against the kitchen ceiling if her mother tells her to grow up and act her age. Of course, she should remove the dough from the ceiling, but she does not need to be told how much of a baby she is or that she will never grow up. Statements such as, "You never learn, do you? You're a big girl now, and big girls don't do stupid things like that," will not help the daughter to mature. Being asked to take responsibility for her carelessness and being expected to correct any damage will help her to mature. It is an enigma of living with teen-agers that yesterday one was too mature to throw pizza dough; tomorrow one will be too mature to throw pizza dough, but today one threw pizza dough. Today one is not too mature for the antics of a seven-year-old child.

What to Expect When Company Comes

There is nothing wrong with requiring the same behavior from a child in the presence of guests that is normally expected. The same responsible behavior should be practiced when guests are visiting in the parents' home as when parents and children are guests in the home of friends. Too many children learn that they can get away with more in guest situations. This undesirable learning need not take place if parents will only function the same in guest situations as they do when at home alone with their children.

The presence of a visitor is an ideal time for a child to test parental limits. When a child tests his or her parents in these guest situations, many parents experience difficulty in exercising the same interactions as they normally would. Parents are frequently afraid that friends will think badly of them if they do and say the same things in the presence of others that they do when they are alone with the children.

Mothers and fathers fear that they will be perceived as nagging, tyrannical, or overly harsh parents if they mention some inappropriate behavior to one of their children in front of nonfamily members. If they say no to a child's request, they think it will make them seem excessively harsh. Because of this excessive parental fear of what others will think, children quickly learn to make requests in the presence of nonfamily members that they would never ask for when alone with their parents.

Parents become embarrassed when a child exercises irresponsible behavior or makes unreasonable requests in the presence of others, but parents can be saved this embarrassment once their child learns that unreasonable behavior will not be tolerated and unreasonable requests will not be honored. To accomplish this, parents must first learn to reduce their fear of what others may think and say. They must continue to respond in the same consistent manner that they use when alone with their children. Unacceptable behavior and unreasonable requests will become less frequent and eventually will be dropped to the same level that prevails in the absence of guests.

It is inadvisable in fact to be overly permissive in front of friends and then come down hard on children when the guests leave or when the family returns home. Such a facade is readily detected by children and undermines their respect for their parents. Any concern that parents plan to address regarding their children's behavior can be made in a concise nonthreatening manner while guests are present. In this way, children learn to associate the parental response directly with the behavior on their part that caused the response. A parent's response will not be so embarrassing to the child if it is a normal, expected response—a response that would have been expected under any conditions. When the parents maintain an even level of expectations, a child learns to maintain the same behavior in the presence of third parties that is exercised when alone with parents.

Viewpoint Differences

Parents can expect to have quite different views from their teenagers on a variety of subjects. At times there may be radical differences. As children move into their early teen-aged years, they care much more about what their peers think than they care about what their parents think. This is a normal process that parents should grow to expect from children. Disregard for parental opinion certainly does not need encouragement, but it should be tolerated.

A teen-ager can be permitted to have his or her view, but when it leads to behavior that is outside the parental limits, it does become the parent's problem. But only then is parental intervention indicated.

Unreasonable Expectations of Parents

The temptation to give children additional attention when they are ill should be considered an unrealistic expectation. Children do not inherit the expectation for additional attention when they are ill; they learn it from their parents. Additional attention to an ill child in the form of furnishing amusement and granting frequent desires can encourage the child to be ill more frequently. This is one way of getting extra attention. A child should be getting a reasonable amount of parental attention all along when he or she is well. It should not be necessary to have to wait until illness strikes for parents to be concerned enough to devote their time to their children. Excessive attention when ill can lead to excessive illness. When they become adults, these children are likely to become hypochondriacs, especially if periods of illness were the only occasions when parental attention was forthcoming on the child's terms.

The best way to reduce a child's unreasonable bids for attention during illness or upon the occasion of a minor accident is to ignore them. Before I am accused of being cold and heartless, I need to reiterate that of course a child's genuine health and safety needs must be met. The key lies in realistically interpreting what is genuine and what requests are reasonable. The point is that more parents tend to be overly attending upon occasions of minor accidents and illnesses than vice versa. Parents can be the primary change agents in these situations by refusing to reward their children's unrealistic expectations.

Working Mothers

One woman started a beauty salon in her home because she did not want her children to have to come home to an empty house. Her reasoning was as follows: The family needed additional income, and her entry into the work force appeared to be the only solution. This did mean that the children would be unsupervised for several hours each day after school—unless she could work in her own home. The woman eliminated consideration of all jobs that would require her to be away from home. Several areas of her vocational interest were eliminated because they could not be converted to a stay-at-home job. Finally the decision was made to break ground in a totally new profession in which mother had no training—hair styling. Every day for six months, she diligently attended hair styling classes—all so she could set up shop at home so the children would not have to come home to an empty house.

Yet what is so bad about junior high and high school students coming home to an empty house? Furthermore it is unrealistic for many parents to quit work or set up shop at home just so an adult can be in attendance with the children at all times. In the actual case just cited, it might actually have been better if the children had come home to an empty house; for, as it was, these children came home to a house filled with overwatchfulness and mistrust. The overwatchfulness was manifested by the mother's requirement that the children keep their bedroom doors open at all times so she could supervise them. The mistrust was exemplified by such things as the mother rummaging through their closets and dresser drawers while they were at school. If anything was misplaced, she was quick to call it to their attention as soon as they returned from school. She was also suspicious of any new or unfamiliar items the children stashed in their rooms.

Most parents do not function as this mother did, but nevertheless they feel a need to be available to supervise the children whenever they are home. Children do not expect (and, in fact, may resent) this kind of overinvolvement with parents, and parents have no need to expect this kind of overinvolvement of themselves. Often such parents are simply responding to their perception of what others expect of them.

Overloaded Circuits

In families where ambitions run high, a propensity exists to set a great number of difficult goals for family members. The pace is usually established by acquisitive parents who seek to be upwardly mobile economically and socially. This sometimes leads to overloaded circuits for family members who constrain themselves to a rigid time frame. The overloaded circuits referred to are time circuits, intellectual circuits, and emotional circuits.

Time circuits of parents can become clogged with too many activities for a twenty-four hour day. These parents go at breakneck speed as they try to do all the right things on schedule for their children. They expect to accomplish almost every one of their goals immediately.

Intellectual circuit overloaders are bright individuals who have a compulsion to excel in intellectual tasks to the detriment of their own enjoyment, as well as that of their family.

Emotional circuit overloaders are the most prevalent. They are persons who get caught in spiraling self-expectations by setting goals so high that they are frequently disappointed when their self-expectations are not consistently met. Such goals are often justified by tying them to progress or a better standard of living.

Excessive striving and its resulting overloaded circuits is a more common unrealistic parental self-expectation in the United States than it is abroad, perhaps because of the rags-to-riches tradition.

The children of circuit overloaders tend to function in one of two ways: (1) they get caught up in their parents' ambitious life-style and develop overloaded circuits of their own or (2) they see no way to win, so they then withdraw from the race into an antiacquisitive world—a world where they can espouse the antithesis of the previous generations' values. Much unhappiness and disappointment could be avoided if more parents would set realistic self-expectations and worry less about meeting tedious expectations.

Predictable Parents

Once my daughter Tammy and a neighbor child were playing in our house within my hearing when I noted that all was not going well between them. It seems that they had gotten several pencils from my desk to draw with. The neighbor child decided to call some of the pencils her own and announced her plans to take them home. Tammy warned her to put the pencils back and reminded the girl that the pencils belonged to her father. She must have come on quite strong with her verbal assertions because her friend said, "Well, I'll tell your daddy." Tammy replied, "Go ahead and tell him. He won't do anything." That was how I learned that she knew what to expect of me. She knew that I would not automatically side with the other child and chide my own daughter about the disagreement. She also knew that the strong assertive statements she had used to get the girl to return the pencils would not be condemned, because they were justified and necessary to correct the incident.

Parents sometimes feel an obligation to be the prosecutor of their own children when situations such as this arise in the presence of others. Tammy was right in refusing to be intimidated by the other girl, and she was right in her assumption that I would do nothing. Incidentally, the pencils were returned to the desk, and the neighbor girl never again tried to pit daughter and father against one another. Parents need to stop any automatic condemnation of behavior when their children are in the presence of others. And when children can predict their parents' responses with a degree of accuracy, they can be more independent and appropriately assertive in their interpersonal relations. Parental predictability offers a kind of security.

What else should children be able to expect from their parents? They should be able to expect sane replies to their requests. This does not mean that an occasional no will not be forthcoming. Children should, however, expect predictable behavior from their parents even more than parents should expect predictable behavior of their children. The ability to anticipate their parents' replies can become a useful skill for children, helping them to learn what things are responsible and reasonable and what things are irresponsible and unreasonable. With time, children will begin to discern requests which are likely to be granted. When children anticipate a negative response to an unreasonable request, they can give themselves an internal response, and the request never gets to the parents. Gradually this allows each parent to react positively on most occasions and to reply with a higher percentage of positive answers. When children reach the middle of the teen years, they will have learned not to expect to turn to their parents for every minor decision.

The importance of the information that parents contribute to a teen-ager's life should be examined. If advice, restriction, or expectation will not be important or relevant to the child, then it is best not given by the parents. Many parents offer insignificant guidance and restrictive inputs. In being allowed to exercise and improve their decision-making powers by being given additional freedom of movement in deciding how to complete a task or how to reach an objective, children can grow into mature adults. They learn to expect less parental involvement, and parents should expect to play a less-involved but supportive role as their children grow older.

Positive Reinforcement

Teen-agers expect, and rightly so, that their parents will comment favorably on specific desirable behaviors and on tasks well done. They do not expect fake flattery, nor do they deserve it. Sincere appreciation based on specific behavioral facts is quite another thing that has nothing to do with flattery.

It is not enough merely to tell a child that certain undesirable behaviors are inappropriate. It is up to the parent to follow through and tell or even demonstrate what specific alternative behaviors might have been more appropriate for a particular occasion. It is a parent's responsibility to let the child know what behaviors are expected. Children have every right to expect their parents to do more than criticize and complain about what they do wrong.

Children expect and should get explanations of what is acceptable and why it is acceptable. They also expect their parents to exemplify the same behavior that parents expect from children.

Parental Value System

For over a decade, parents have been bombarded with child-rearing advice from every imaginable source. Some have overreacted and begun to question the usefulness of their traditional values with those of today's liberated generation. These parents have turned loose of some of their old values, but have failed to replace them with new values. When parents do this, they sometimes leave their chidlren in a value vacuum. Such a vacuum often indicates to children that nothing is worth expending energy on or striving for. Parents do no favor to children when they have strong opinions and fail to defend them or pretend they are not there. Values tend to manifest themselves in various behaviors anyway, even when parents do not verbalize them.

On the other hand, it is unrealistic to expect children to accept every value held by their parents. At best, parental values—even those not accepted by the children—only serve as useful reference points for children. Children have a right to expect their parents to own a value system, and they also have the right to expect to be allowed to develop their own values, even when their values do not fully coincide with those of their parents.

Parents Are Expected to Set Limits

Behavioral limits naturally evolve from parental value systems. Limits do not have to be set in every area of a child's life, because children will often function within a reasonable behavioral range as a normal result of their modeling their parents' behaviors. However, in areas where parental values produce strong feeling, it is appropriate for parents to express these feelings where their children are concerned. This can best be done by setting parental limits. Limits can be set in a broad manner that allows for some behavioral variation. A child needs some breathing room—an opportunity to choose specific courses of action from within the broad range of possibilities lying between the parent's set limits. Children's expectations for parental limits will cause them to abide by a particular limit even if they feel it is overly restrictive, provided they think their parents are reasonable in most of their limit setting.

Parental Apologies

I suspect that apologies to children from parents are few. Children need not expect a parental apology after every unresolved disagreement, but, when a parent has functioned in a manner that is later felt to be inappropriate, it is totally acceptable for the parent to apologize for his or her own behavior. The first parental apology may come as a genuine surprise to a child who is unaccustomed to hearing parental admission of wrongdoing. When it is clear to everyone that a parent's behavior was clearly uncalled for, a child is fully justified in expecting an apology.

10
Mapping a Vocational Route

A parent asked recently, "Why are parents so concerned about what their children will do when they grow up?" This father went on to say that the schools have vocational counseling, interest tests, computerized student-job matching, and numerous other techniques to help each child make a sound vocational choice. What this father did not know is that a great many schools across America today do not have adequate career counseling. He was advised to check with his son and with his son's school to see what steps actually were being taken toward guiding children in their vocational choices.

When I next saw this man, he, too, was concerned about what the school was doing to help his son make an acceptable vocational choice. In his son's school, vocational-interest testing was not being done with all students routinely. Most of the school's assessment activities dealt with achievement testing, much of which was used to predict success in college. All children were not seen individually by a guidance counselor for the purpose of receiving help with their vocational decision making. The father was pleased, however, to learn that his son could take an interest test, but very few of the children were apprised of this opportunity and therefore did not take advantage of it. This father inquired about interest tests and what their usefulness might be. He discussed the most frequently used vocational interest tests, how each is used, and how the interest test interpretation should be integrated with other vocational information such as achievement tests, high school grades, job market forecasts, and the child's own verbalized interests. The usefulness of integrating all this information to help one think in terms of groups of vocations for further consideration instead of separate, individual vocations was explained.

Reducing the Risks of Vocational Choice

Risks are involved in committing oneself to a particular vocation and to the education required to prepare for that vocation. But by not planning at all, an even greater risk is assumed—the risk of getting the left-over jobs.

Furthermore, tomorrow's career reality may well result from today's fantasy. The probability of moving from a childhood fantasy to a future job reality is increased when youth back up their decisions with organized planning, needed sacrifice, and persistent dedication, but this move cannot begin until the risk of frustration and possible failure are evaluated.

Selecting a vocation could even be compared to taking a shot in the dark for those teen-agers who have had little experience in the work world and in decision-making. Certain activities, however, can be used to shed some light on an illusive target. Interest tests reduce the area of uncertainty. If possible, they should be combined with after-school jobs, as well as weekend and summer jobs, obtained by the teen-agers. Such jobs, whatever their nature, offer valuable experience and serve as information-gathering experiments for later career decision making. Not only does a teen-ager benefit by learning particular vocational skills on the job, but more important, social and decision-making skills are developed.

An after-school, weekend, or summer job serves as an inexpensive testing ground that puts a young worker in touch with his or her interests and abilities. A temporary work experience could call attention to the unreality of a youth's career fantasy while simultaneously sparing the career aspirant from an unfortunately large educational or financial commitment to a career destined to result in dissatisfaction or failure. Temporary jobs can also help a teen-ager decide whether or not to go to college and even what to study.

Job experience as a teen-ager does not remove all risks from career decision-making. A youth may follow-up on the decision to attend college and then wash out. School failure, like any other failure, has no note of finality about it. Any amount of college education satisfactorily completed by a student will still be an asset in the work world. In situations involving a recent high school graduate who decides to seek employment instead of going to college, the decision is a reversible one. Additional education can be obtained at any age for most careers. Each person has the right to decide to attend college at a later point in his life or to decide to return to the campus at an older age to seek an advanced degree or to "retool" in an entirely new field. Part-time and temporary employment situations teach teen-agers to exercise self-discipline as they try out their budding decision-making skills. Self-discipline is acquired as they are forced to interact with fellow workers and customers and as they learn to conform to a time structure. It is not uncommon among today's youth to find teen-agers whose career aspirations are not supported with the necessary amount of self-discipline, which could have been generated by temporary or part-time employment, or perhaps through educational achievement. Self-responsibility and self-discipline are attributes that are particularly useful in the areas of vocational decision making and implementation. This is the primary reason that self-responsibility and self-discipline should be supported as part of a child's daily routine beginning as early as preschool. Otherwise the child may become an adult whose unrealistic fantasies have developed into tremendous aspirations that unfortunately are not supported with the experiential information and self-discipline required to reach the goals they generate.

The Parental Role in Vocational Choice

Carlyle said, "Our grand business is not to see what lies dimly at a distance but to do what lies clearly at hand." The task clearly at hand for parents is to support their teen-agers in getting vocational and educational information and experience. This information and experience are to be used by the child, and not by some overinvolved parent for career decision-making. At no point should parents overwork their own decision-making skills in an area that must ultimately be resolved by their children. As children progress into their mid-teen years, parental decision-making must gradually be replaced with a process in which children make their own decisions. The concept of decision-making and the specific steps involved in scientific decision making were discussed in a previous chapter. Children can certainly put this procedure to use by using it when considering career choices. Career decisions are one of the first areas where a youth can practice long-term decision-making.

Some children are predisposed to rely heavily on their parents' career directions. This is seen especially in situations where the children have little other information to draw from. These children would be better served if their parents were used as resources to guide them to additional career information sources and to particular individuals already in professions of possible interest. More teen-agers should use career professionals as resources to acquire additional needed information. Persons other than parents, who are in particular vocational fields, can frequently comment more objectively than can parents—even those in the field under consideration.

Much of the information from parents and others in particular vocations is subjective. As such, this material should not be thought of as absolute truths but, rather, as subjective information to be considered in light of the context from which it originated. For example, a child would need to rethink the positive assertions of an attorney father who fantasizes having his child as a future law partner. A biologist aunt who has just been layed off after ten years with the same company could be expected to speak of the profession in less glowing terms than would a biologist neighbor who has just been promoted to director of research.

Teen-agers need someone to provide them with useful guidelines in assessing the wealth of subjective career information. This could be an adult outside the immediate family to whom the youth is attracted—someone who shows a particular interest in the youth. If an older teen-ager happens to establish a temporary mentor relationship with a mature adult in a profession of interest, parents would be wise to remain unthreatened by the relationship. Rather they should welcome the mentor as an additional resource to help with the parenting task in the area of vocational choice.

It is common to see parents, especially fathers, direct their teen-age children toward the profession that the parents chose for themselves decades earlier. And while most parents should be in a position to speak knowledgeably about their own professions, they will have great difficulty in being objective. Parents need to be especially careful not to live out their own unfulfilled vocational dreams through their children by projecting their unmet aspirations onto their children.

A parent might be able to give a child an initial boost into the profession of the parent's choice. The well-informed parent could spare the child some of the pitfalls that the parent had experienced earlier in his or her own career. This parental boost might, however, be dysfunctional in two respects: (1) children are denied a significant portion of their learning experience when they are steered around obstacles by a more experienced parent, and (2) children's natural interests and inate abilities may lie in a different area that could remain completely untapped if they find themselves locked into the profession of their parents' choice. This can readily result in a situation where an individual becomes, for example, a third-rate nurse when he or she might have become a first-rate physicist.

Career Satisfaction

Children, even throughout their teen-age years, continue to have some wide-eyed, unrealistic daydreams about their future career accomplishments. This is partially due to not having yet experienced the practical details of carrying out plans in the work world. They have not experienced the repeated frustrations of unexpected disappointments, nor have opportunities been suddenly snatched from their grasp.

Highly organized, achievement oriented teen-agers and young adults tend to plan their careers many years into the future. Still, planning of this type cannot take into consideration the feedback information that an individual can obtain as he or she progresses along a particular career route. It cannot take into consideration future changes in the economy, job obsolescence, or technologies that are yet to be developed, which may expand some professions along new and unexpected routes while completely curtailing other professions.

Long-range goals, while useful, serve better when they are general rather than specific. It is possible to develop a specific, long-range goal that looked attractive ten years earlier—a goal pursued with much diligence and persistence by carefully staying off all interesting side tracks. Unfortunately, such single-mindedness can lead an individual right past terrific opportunities and right past areas of even greater interest where more inate abilities could have been used. The result may be an individual who has been successful in obtaining a specific career objective at the expense of being just as unsuccessful in obtaining career satisfaction. Long-range career goals are useful so long as they are not compulsively pursued right past more satisfying activities in which the individual could have been equally successful. There is something to be said for enjoying a goal while it is being pursued *and* when it is achieved. Career satisfaction is not automatically assured upon attainment of career goals that were established a decade earlier.

11
Termination of Parenting—Continuation of Friendship

Letting go of children emotionally is torture for some parents. These are the parents who have clung to their children out of their own strong need to be needed. Their relationship with their children is as clinging when the child is nineteen as it was at nine-years or even at nine months. Psychological distancing from their children is unusually anxiety-provoking for such parents, and it produces anxiety in their children as well. This situation will never materialize in your home if you let loose of your children in a gradual manner, starting at an early age, say, age five. Letting loose means allowing your child to solve some of his or her own problems, even at kindergarten age.

So many things in the human environment are simply neither black nor white, although some persons operate on the premise that they are. More frequently, situations fall on a continuum somewhere between the two extremes. The concept of child guidance is best thought of as a continuum that can vary from the extreme of complete parental planning of every detail of a child's present and future life with no thought for the child's desires to the other extreme of total nonintervention. As the children grow older, parents should find themselves moving along this continuum from a position of nearly total planning for a baby toward a position approaching nearly complete nonintervention by age eighteen.

The Communication Gap

The more explicit and the less implicit communication that is exchanged across the generations between parent and child the better the relationship is for all involved. Implicit communication is a gray area of informational overlap as shown in Figure 1 while explicit communication is an aboveboard informational overlap spelled out in black and white for all to see (see Figure 2). With explicit communication there is no guessing about the intent of child/parent messages.

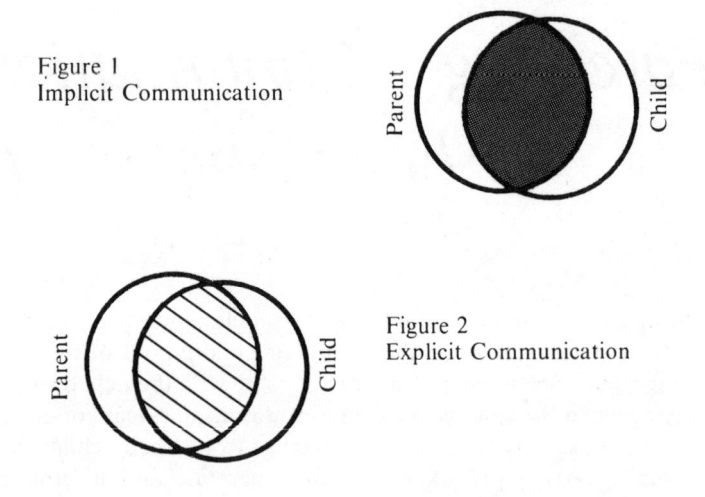

Figure 1
Implicit Communication

Figure 2
Explicit Communication

Note that the same amount of communication exists in both figures, that is, the quantity of communications is the same. To point out the need for explicit communications in no way should be taken to mean that there will be total communication between children and parents. Sometime during the early teen years, most children begin to reduce the amount of communication they share with their parents. Particular subjects such as sex may fade from the conversation first. Later an increasing number of topics become off limits.

No harm is done by parents who sit back and allow this more restrictive communication pattern to happen, while plenty of harm can be done by parents who pry into the now off limits subject areas. Parents do not have to know everything that is going on with a teenager, just as teen-agers have no need to know all the details of their parents' lives. A mother and her six-year-old child, who have an eighty percent overlap in their total communication worlds, will be right on target when the child reaches sixteen if they are then functioning at forty percent or lower communication overlap. Even spouses should not strive for more than a ninety-five percent overlap of communications. No one benefits from relationships where total communication sharing exists, because complete thought sharing approaches ownership, and no one wants to be owned by another individual. Examples of appropriate communication sharing are shown below:

Figure 3
70-95 percent
Husband/Wife

Figure 4
60-80 percent
Parent/Child (6 years)

Figure 5
25-40 percent
Parent/Child (16 years)

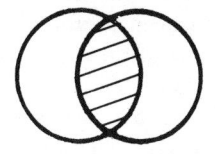

Have you ever seen parents who try to be a peer to their children—try to do everything their children do and be wherever they are. Some of these parents are trying to keep themselves from growing older, and in some way, associating with their children makes them feel younger. Still other parents think that their children expect it of them. They believe that behaving youthfully has something to do with being a good parent. Perhaps these parents are rewarded when someone outside the family says, "Oh, look at those parents. They just do everything with their kids."

I will not go so far as to say the cliche "familiarity breeds contempt" is totally true, but the few parents who do have excessive amounts of time available to spend with children need to avoid the tendency to do so. Certainly no mother or father should communicate with his or her children to the extent that the children's same-age friends are excluded. "Play, then go your way" is a motto worth remembering for the hovering, ever-present parent. Constant companionship in no way makes children more accepting or respectful of parents.

Forming Close Friendships Outside the Family

As they grow older, if children communicate less with their parents, does this mean that they share less communication with everyone? Not at all. Children need to become increasingly communicative with same-aged friends. Peers begin to take up part of the communications and social interaction slack left by the reduced quantity (but not quality) of parental communications. Most children have no problem with this, and some parents comment that their children would gladly associate with peers all the time, if allowed to.

Yet, there are other children who tend to remain isolated—to be loners. Such children may need parental encouragement to become more socially active; however, direct techniques such as parental verbalizations to this effect are seldom effective in stimulating needed social interaction. Further the parental need to be needed sometimes discourages parents from encouraging children to put peers on an equal level with parents. Once this natural parental resistance is overcome, parents of loners can help clear away roadblocks to the child's peer interactions.

Some of these roadblocks may have been erected by a child who has grown fearful of entering social situations with minimal social skills. In this case, social skills can be casually discussed.

The parent who has enjoyed a young child who has readily shared confidences may feel as if the rug had been pulled from under this once mutually satisfying relationship. This is most threatening to the parent who learns that his older child has begun sharing intimate information with a peer but not with mom or dad, as used to be the case. This confiding of feelings and aspirations among children, however, is a prime example of allowing children to pull away a little—to reduce the quantity of parent/child communications, to individuate.

Security

Some parents experience difficulty in turning loose their children because they want to protect them from the insecurities that life imposes. Such parents may suffer from an excessive fear of insecurity themselves. This has caused them to operate their life space in such a way as to eliminate all sources of insecurity. They want to do the same for their children. But consider these words by Helen Keller:

Security is mostly a superstition. It does not exist in nature nor do the children of men as a whole experience it. Avoiding danger is no safer in the long run than out-right exposure. Life is either a daring adventure or nothing.

Security is not a commodity that can be purchased in so many units. Security does not come from without but is generated from within an individual; it is an individual's ability to deal effectively with his or her environment. If you insist on giving your children more security than you had, then give them learning experiences that enable them to deal more effectively with their environment.

What good does it do to tell a child to be careful every time he or she leaves the house for a few minutes? This just lowers the child's self-image without giving any help to the child in knowing what is required to be careful. The implicit message to the child is, "Dad doesn't think I will be careful. He thinks he has to watch me every minute. He doesn't trust me behind his back." Perhaps there really are specific dangers to be avoided. If there are, they should be mentioned, along with precautionary actions that the child should take in dealing with each one. If the dangers have already been called to a child's attention on an earlier occasion, it is time to remain silent, provided the child has demonstrated the necessary competence in handling the dangers on the earlier occasion. If a child has shown an inability to cope with the possibly dangerous environment, then the parent should not allow the child to be exposed to the situation again until additional learning is acquired. Parents have an obligation to say no when no is the best answer for a child's safety.

At age eight my son asked to be allowed to ride his bike to his grandmother's house, which was two miles, nine intersections, and one railroad crossing away. Although his total bike-riding experience was limited, permission was granted after he and I discussed the traffic laws pertaining to bicycles. He was told how to be alert for the objects and events in his bicycle-riding environment, namely automobiles, and how to make good use of his senses of sight and hearing. The special precaution of stopping completely at a particular intersection and at the railroad crossing were mentioned. Appropriate alternative behaviors were mentioned regarding several contingencies that could develop—contingencies such as a bicycle breakdown or a passer-by offering him a ride. All this took less than ten minues. A last-minute reminder from me that responsible behavior was expected came in the form of the statement, "Rick, promise me you won't run over any cars. It makes the drivers awfully mad to get hit by a bicycle." His response was something like, "Yeah,

I wouldn't want to make any drivers mad." A safe trip and a fun visit were the results of this excursion. This boy is now sixteen years old, and his cycling skills have expanded to fifty-mile bike-a-thon trips. Next is the century—a one-hundred-mile organized bicycle excursion. Any security in his present bicycling activities comes not from his father but from his having properly functioning equipment and from his skill in handling this equipment.

Parents sometimes ask their children to be careful in situations having risks comparable to those in the bicycle incident without first taking positive actions to lessen the danger. Parents should give their chidren the learning experiences they need to cope with hazards that cannot be eliminated. And when the children show that they can handle themselves in hazardous or difficult situations, it is immediately time to accentuate this positive behavior by encouraging them with verbal reinforcements.

What about the long-range security that a few children try to guarantee for themselves by remaining attached to their parents— even after the children have passed through adolescense into adulthood? There is no long-range security in clinging to a parent who is twenty to thirty years older and, who will, according to the laws of probability, die thirty years before the son or daughter. Individuals who have not been allowed to mature as they pass into adulthood are vulnerable to inevitable disappointments from loss of love objects. With the parent dies the cherished security, or rather, the feeling of security that should have been set aside decades earlier.

Teen-Aged Drivers

Why do teen-agers have poorer driving records than adult drivers do? One reason is because teen-age drivers are necessarily new drivers and as such have not had the opportunity to fine-tune their driving skills. Most teen-agers would never admit that their parents are better drivers than they are, but more times than not a parent will be a better driver in a pinch than a sixteen-year-old will be. A parents reaction time might be a fraction of a second slower, but his or her perceptiveness of possible road hazards, the processing of complex stimuli, and psychomotor coordination probably exceed those of teen-agers.

Other than experience, the things that help a teen-ager's driving record are: (1) trust; (2) early and steadily increasing assumption of a wide variety of responsibilities; (3) knowledge by the child that he or she will be allowed to experience the logical consequences of his or her driving behavior; and (4) increasing withdrawal of parental control over a broad spectrum of parent-child involvements. The lessening of parental control should have progressed to the point where the sixteen-year-old gets most of his or her control messages internally—to the point where external parental controls are rarely needed.

The need of the older teen-ager to exercise control is sometimes met in a destructive way when that teen-ager is a frustrated licensed driver who has no other outlets to exercise control other than behind the wheel of a car. If the teen-ager feels a need to demonstrate this control to peers, the car and driver essentially become an accident looking for some place to happen. A speeding car may represent the first time that some teen-agers have had to exercise any degree of control without parental intervention. The parent who has increasingly withdrawn and allowed his or her child to gradually assume more control has much less reason to stay awake nights waiting for the child to return with the family car in one piece. And, of course, even less concern is needed if the child has completed a good driver's training course; has parental trust with the car, as well as with other matters; and has built up a large, varied repertoire of responsibilities that have been satisfactorily assumed.

Freedom to Fail

Civil libertarians are vigilant in their efforts to protect the basic freedoms they see as being inherent for all people. Few persons, however, support the cause of "freedom to fail," which should be regarded as a basic right of all citizens. When there is always a rescuer to keep us from avoiding the natural and logical consequences of our behaviors, we are denied a basic freedom—freedom to fail. Children also need to experience this freedom as the great rescuers (parents) pull back from their former watchfulness and frequent interventions.

"I don't want my kids to make the same mistakes I did," is a fairly common expression and attitude among parents who deny their children the freedom to fail. As children become older and assume ever increasing responsibility for their lives, they are bound to experience occasional failures among their successes. Parents who can regard their children's failures as temporary frustrations are in the fortunate position to convey to their children that failure can serve a useful purpose—it can be a learning experience. On the other hand, most of the time children know when they have failed, and they do not need to be reminded of it, as is too often the case, by ever-present parents. Neither do they need a parent who says, "I would rather do it myself; you can't do anything right." Inducing guilt in children for causing their parents grief over a failure is something to guard against. Being made to feel bad or guilty for not measuring up is a sure way to stifle maturation of the responsibility-assuming process.

Money—The Great Dependency Maker

Children become more independent when they do not have to come to mother or father for money every time they need to buy something. Allowances serve the useful purpose of permitting children to have money to spend as they see the need. As such, they are useful in helping children learn the use of money, how to get value in their purchases, and how to save for later needs. Children are inclined to learn useful money management more quickly if they are required to earn their allowance. Allowance earners seek to make their money work harder for them if they have had to work hard for it. It is not uncommon to see a child equating a mowed lawn with so many candy bars or a weekend of supermarket check-out earnings to an equivalent number of movie admissions.

All school-aged children need some of their own money to spend, and they need more of it as they grow older. The purchasing of goods and services by parents for use by the children should fade from the scene as the children advance to their early teen-aged years. This procedure is best replaced with situations where parents give money to their children with sufficient guidelines and trust to allow the children to make many of their own purchases. As children advance still further into teen years they will, one hopes, become more fully independent by earning much of the money that they spend to meet their needs. Ideally, they are deferring gratitude on larger purchases until the time when their saved earnings makes such purchases possible.

The reduced need to turn to parents for money has a major impact on the process of allowing children to individuate from their parents. By high school graduation, parents should buy only the more costly, strictly essential needs for their children, and all other needs should be met with purchases made by the children.

Independence

Parents may feel threatened when their children show independent behavior. It is uncomfortable to realize that one's children can make decisions and do things without the parents' helping hand. Fortunately, most children will eventually achieve this needed feeling of independence from their parents with or without parental approval. It is much better if independence is achieved as a result of the parents having turned loose. When parents do not turn loose, the child may attain independence anyway by repeatedly frustrating the objectives that the parents have established for the child.

Parents who have trouble turning loose are vulnerable to being manipulated by their children. The children may threaten to withhold love from their parents unless the parents continue to do as the children wish. Since distancing and loss of love are the things that these parents fear most, they are prone to comply with any and all requests made by their children, whether or not they are reasonable. Parents who comply with unreasonable requests have usually functioned in a manner that has encouraged their children to make such requests. One of the best examples of encouraging dependent behavior was seen in Lonnie, age twenty.

> Lonnie had been sickly much of his life, and his mother used this as a reason to wait on him. At meals Lonnie asked his mother to cut his meat, and his mother would graciously do it for him.
> Each morning Lonnie's clothes were neatly laid out for him in just the order needed to put them on. Lonnie's mother had been a frequent visitor at the local public schools every year since her son entered the first grade. She made certain that the teachers and administration knew that her son was special. They must understand that he needed special attention due to his many illnesses, that he needed individual help with his learning problems, and that not as much could be expected of him. Attending vocational school was no big problem for Lonnie, because his mother was again on hand to explain all the special circumstances that surrounded her son. Selecting drafting tools was no problem for Lonnie because his mother selected and bought them herself.
> It will be years before anyone will ever know what Lonnie can do. He has never had to do anything on his own that might have taxed his physical or mental strength. At present no one has much of an idea about Lonnie's capabilities. He and his mother might be genuinely surprised at what he could accomplish. But first, a considerable amount of letting go by his mother must take place before Lonnie can even begin to catch up.

How many Lonnies are there in the world today, and what are their ages? There are too many Lonnies, and their ages range from eight to eighty. Each of us as parents can do our part by insuring that there are no Lonnies under our roofs. The process of turning loose is least painful when it is started in kindergarten and allowed to progress gradually until the child leaves the parents' home. As children get older, they regard their parents' offers of frequent help as efforts to overly control their lives. Ideally, the child of possessive parents will perceive the parents' efforts for what they are and reject them.

Measuring Independence

Most parents have some idea about the degree of independence in their children. Their idea may or may not be correct. An objective measure of independence is needed. By turning back to Chapter 7, which contains a discussion of responsibility, the reader can calculate an objective independence score using the list of 101 age-appropriate responsibilities. There are other measures of independence, but since responsibility is an appreciable part of the concept of independence, the 101 age-appropriate responsibility list is a worthwhile tool to use in measuring a child's independence. Use the following four-step formula in making calculations:

> 1. Note the total number of responsibilities on the cumulative list corresponding to the child's age. This is the child's maximum possible raw score.
> 2. Subtract 1 point for each age-appropriate responsibility that the child does not perform. Subtract 2 points for each responsibility the child does not do for the next younger year. Subtract 3 points for responsibilities not routinely done at the two years younger age level, and so on until you work back to the first item on the list, *Put napkins on table for meals*, listed under *The two-year old Can*.
> 3. Subtract the points in Step 2 from the total possible raw score in Step 1.
> 4. Divide the actual raw score obtained in step 3 by the total possible raw score in Step 1 and multiply by 100. This is the Percent Independence Score.

The Percent Independence Score can be anything from 100 percent to a negative score. Anything above 50 percent is satisfactory, although ideally scores should be above 75 percent. Not only does the Percent Independence Score provide an objective numerical approximation of a child's independence, but the items on the list at and below the child's age serve as examples of specific responsibilities that the child can start acquiring.

> Example 1: A three-year-old child does 6 of the 10 things appropriate for his/her age and 7 of the 8 things appropriate for a two-year-old child.
>
> Step 1.   18 items
>
> Step 2.   Cannot do 3 items appropriate for a three-year-old = -3
> Cannot do 1 item appropriate for a two-year-old = -2

Step 3. 18-5 = 13

Step 4. 13/18 x 100 = 72 percent = Percent Independence Score

Example 2: A brand new teen-ager (thirteen years old) can do half of the items listed for a thirteen-year-old, 5 things appropriate for a twelve-year-old, 3 things appropriate for an eleven-year-old, 6 things for a ten-year-old and all of the things listed for children ages two through nine.

Step 1. 95 items

Step 2. Cannot do 2 items appropriate for a thirteen-year-old = -2
Cannot do 2 items appropriate for a twelve-year-old = -4
Cannot do 3 items appropriate for an eleven-year-old = -9
Cannot do 1 item appropriate for a ten-year-old = -4
-19

Step 3. 95 - 19 = 76

Step 4. 76/95 x 100 = 80 percent = Percent Independence Score

Overidentifying with Children

All individuals lower their defenses and open themselves for attack when they wrap their whole lives up in any one thing. Perhaps a few people can handle this, but most of us need a variety of interests to occupy our time and resources. It is more common to find fathers absorbed in their work, while mothers are usually overly involved with the children. Yet, the primary relationship for a wife should be with her husband, and the husband's primary relationship should be with his wife. A man's wife will remain an important part of his environment when his job is separated from his life by retirement, and a woman's husband will still be there when all the children have left home and her job as mother is finished. The woman who is no longer needed in the role of dedicated mother is a too-frequent client in the psychologist's office.

Parents whose lives focus entirely on their children find it difficult to relate to their children objectively. Overly dedicated parents find themselves frequently taking sides with their own children, thinking they can do no wrong. Many of these parents martyr themselves for their children by doing all within their power to ensure the child's happiness. Martyred parents often come to feel that childrearing is a cross to bear, and they cannot truthfully think of parenthood as an opportunity that could and should be enjoyed. They continue to show others how they persevere against great odds and thereby draw much pity to themselves.

Parents do not have to be engaged in every aspect of a child's life. A good disengagement program begins when the child enters kindergarten and is essentially completed by the time the child completes the teen-age years. When mothers and fathers fail to disengage, they can easily overload their circuits as they add their children's problems to their own problems. Parents with overloaded circuits make ineffective parents who are no fun to be around.

Parents can rightfully take pride in the achievements of their children, but this does not carry the concept far enough. In addition, parents should have achievements of their own in which they take pride. This is necessary so the parents will not get all their feelings of achievement by vicariously living their children's lives.

I know a cemetery manager who has three sons. If you ask him how things are going, he will spring into action and tell you that things are going fine—with his sons. He can tell you about the son who has a Ph.D., the son who is a doctor, and the son who is making straight A's in electrical engineering at an Ivy League university. He can tell you how he has planned their education and how he has planned their careers with careful precision. He arranged for one of them to be employed in his hometown so that father and son could continue their close relationship. The father drives over to the son's house just about every afternoon. With each trip the father sees some new task that the son ought to get done. This son, who teaches sociology in college, could probably run his household without his father's help, but his father still thinks of him as a little boy who must be cared for and protected.

The son is not especially happy in his work at the university, but he felt a strong sense of duty to accept the job offer that his father had arranged for him through local political leaders who had influence with the university selection committee. His father made it appear that only an ingrate would refuse the job offer after all his father had done to help him.

The son who is a physician lives in a distant town that, unfortunately, is not out of telephone reach of the posessive father, who calls twice weekly to ascertain the latest developments with this son's family. The father offers words of wisdom concerning the thirty-two year old doctor's career, his wife's spending habits, and their childrearing practices in return for news of the latest developments in the physician's household. As one might have guessed, it was the father who had originally decided that this son would be a doctor and who pushed for his acceptance to medical school. But it is not the father who now has to live with the son; it is the son's wife. She is feeling pressured by a husband who does not like his work and who feels he must constantly keep nagging his wife so she will live up to the standards that his father has established for her.

Here is a father who has never learned to relinquish control and turn his children loose. The youngest son refuses to play the father's games now, but two years of weekly psychotherapy sessions were required to bring him to this point after this son experienced an intense anxiety neurosis while in high school. This son came through the experience a little scarred but a lot wiser. He has achieved the needed insight and strength to run his life independent of excessive parental guidance.

You Want the Best for Your Child, Don't You?

What a time for a life insurance salesman to call. I was in the shower. We were going out. The baby was crying. The sitter had not come. The salesman said he had sent a card saying he would call on us at this particular time. I did not remember any card. Oh, well, he was here at our apartment, and I did have a few minutes. He must have seen the birth announcement in the newspaper.

The sales call seemed to be going slowly—slowly for me because I was ready for the salesman to leave—slowly for him because he was getting no closer to closing a sale. As I ushered him to the door as politely as possible, he dropped a real sizzler on me from his reservoir of canned sales pitches, "You do want the best for your child, don't you?" I mumbled some kind of incoherent response. The statement had angered me. I considered it intimidating.

That was fifteen years ago. Finally I have worked out an answer. Come back, Mr. Salesman, and I will answer your question, No! As you and the other ninety-five percent of consumer-happy Americans define best, I do not want the best for my child. I cannot afford it. What is more, my child cannot afford it either.

How could anyone say that they are willing to settle for less than the best for their children? Yet I doubt that either my children or your children will always be able to buy what they want when they want it for their entire adult lives. So why should parents teach children to expect always to have all their needs met as soon as the needs are identified? The best for my children involves teaching them to settle for less than the so-called best. The best for my children is helping them to become acquainted with a little frustration and disappointment so that, when these inevitable unwelcome guests pay a visit during their adult years, my children will have developed some coping skills with which to greet them. If I cannot provide my children with something more valuable than money and money-equivalent goods and services, I deserve to feel like the inadequate parent the salesman tried to make me out to be. If I, as a parent, cannot apply some of the parenting principles in this book and convey some of the broad learning experiences emphasized, there is no way I can ever make up for it with insurance policies, toys, clothes, encyclopedias, braces, schools, cars, or any other consumer product or service. No, I do not want the best for my children.

Happiness

Parents do not have to perform like circus clowns to know every trick—to keep their children always smiling. Life as an adult is such that smiles, happiness, and joy are not always available in plentiful amounts. Children are done a great injustice by the parent who tries to always keep them happy, for such children are in for a rude awakening when the real world is introduced to them as adults.

Learning about the world one lives in should be a gradual process that allows time for feedback and corrective behavioral adjustment to the environment. Happiness is achieved as a result of successful daily living, and it should not be sought as a goal in itself. Those who want their children to be happy need to teach them to function effectively as agents for useful change in their world. Parents who would have happy children must not try to legislate happiness into their children's lives, but must continue to turn them loose and to give them the needed freedom to pursue happiness as independent individuals.

12
Conclusion

No psychologist can take all the frustration out of parenting. Every parent has probably felt as Mark Twain must have when he said, "If you pick up a starving dog and make him prosperous, he will not bite you. This is the principal difference between a dog and a man." Who can guarantee that children will not turn on parents after they have done all that appeared necessary to make those children prosperous? Moreover, individual instances that bring about parental pain should not be taken too hard. An occasional act of revenge by a child who feels hurt due to some parental action should not come as a total surprise to parents. It is best to balance out instances of revenge and ingratitude with instances of thoughtfulness and gratitude so that the total experience of parenthood yields a net positive experience.

Elbert Hubbard said, "The greatest mistake you can make in life is to be continually fearing you will make one." The simple fact of being a parent assures one of making a multitude of mistakes. Much parental heartache can be avoided by not expecting perfection from oneself or from one's children. Being an effective parent consists of taking steps in the correct direction, that is, making improvements, however small, on one's present situation.

I remember a family who brought their fifteen-year-old son for therapy. The parents were so insistent on conveying all the boy's misbehaviors to me that I wrote the problems down—all twelve of them. In the course of the third therapy session, I asked the parents if they had noticed any change in their son. They replied, "No. None whatever. He is just as bad as ever." At this point, we looked over the misbehavior list item by item. When the status of each behavior was carefully examined, six items were found in which the son showed slight but definite improvements. The unrealistic expectation of moving from disaster to perfection had somehow eluded parents and child alike.

These parents also suffered from the typical problem of imputing badness onto their child's overall character, based on a few simple instances of misbehavior. They had to learn to deal with the event, not the child. This they learned to do by accepting their son while not accepting certain of his behaviors. They also had to learn to recognize their boy's many appropriate behaviors, which had been occurring all along. The appropriate behaviors occurred in the midst of misbehaviors that had masked the acceptable behaviors from the parents' recognition.

At this point, these parents still had a long way to go. Still, the stage had been set for much-needed change. With this family, as with many others, the change was slow, difficult, and uneven, and there were some periods of regression. After six months of treatment, neither child nor parent had achieved perfection, although enough appreciable positive change had occurred to make the effort worthwhile for all concerned.

In their efforts to appear to have attained perfection, parents may function in one way in front of their children while acting like different people when the children are not around. Parents should have the same standards in the presence of their children as they have when the children are absent. It is time for mothers and fathers to avoid trying to be something they are not for the children's sake. Children need to know that their parents are fallible. By all means, parents should not deny mistakes to their children when they are fortunate enough to be aware of their own shortcomings.

As you begin to think in terms of being the ideal parent, do not fool yourself into believing that total perfection for self or children is mandatory. Parents regularly fall short of being perfect and then go ahead to function in facilitive ways to rear their children to adulthood with the ability to make positive contributions to their society.

A parental apology does not cause children to disrespect their parents; rather, a sincere apology from parent to child commands respect. The individual who recognizes his or her mistakes, admits them, and seeks to correct them has proceded a long way toward becoming a facilitive, respected person. Earned respect and parental perfection do not of necessity go hand-in-hand. Perhaps children would be more accepting of parental mistakes if parents were the first to admit fallibility.

Learning to Do Nothing

There will be occasions for all parents from time to time when it is not at all clear what action should be taken. In these instances no action often proves to be best. By doing nothing, parents go on record as expecting their children to possess the capacity for dealing with their own problems. This is not always the most pleasant way to teach children to assume responsibility for themselves, but children have a way of finding their own solutions for problems when their parents are slow to take action, and doing nothing is definitely an effective way to apply the learning principle of natural consequences.

When Parents Can't Handle Their Children

What options do parents have when problems with their children become overwhelming, and it is clear that doing nothing could prove disastrous? Any time a clear-cut course of appropriate action is urgently needed but manages to elude parents, it is time to seek professional intervention.

Professional intervention could come in one of several forms: (1) most communities have community mental health centers that provide the services of professionals such as psychologists, psychiatrists, and social workers at fees based on the client's ability to pay; (2) many colleges and universities have counseling centers or psychological clinics that treat children and their parents; (3) most telephone directory "yellow pages" have listings for helping professionals—look under (1) psychologist, (2) marriage and family counselors, and (3) physicians and surgeons—psychiatry. Most professionals can determine from one telephone call if a problem is of sufficient intensity to require professional intervention. A professional can tell if the problem is close enough to his or her specialty to justify an appointment, and most professionals who feel the problem is not within the range of his or her competencies will readily refer the inquirer to a more appropriate source of help.

Index

Accidents, 3, 32, 33, 78
Achievement, 120
Advice, children's, 19, 20, 65
Albrecht, Margaret, 74
Alcoholism, 39
Allowances, money, 69, 116
Ambition, 97, 98
Answers, parental, 64, 65
Apologies, parental, 100, 101
Aspirations, parental, 92
Attitude, 12

Begging, 63, 66
Behavior
  goal-oriented, 62, 63
  poor-little-me, 77
  repertoire, 58
Best, providing the, 121
Blame, 20, 74
Blanton, Smiley, 18
Bus catching, 79

Car, family, 62, 63, 84-86
Career
  decisions, 104-7
  planning, 107
  satisfaction, 107
Carlyle, 105
Chores, 69, 71-74
Clock, alarm, 79
Communication
  explicit, 80, 110
  implicit, 80, 110
  modeling, 36
  turn-offs, 15-18
Communication gap, 110
Comparison, sibling, 10
Compliments, 10
Computer mother, 57
Conformity, 59
Consequences
  limitations of, 28, 29
  logical, definition of, 29-31
  natural, definition of, 28, 29
Contingency planning, 75

Control
  excessive, 86
  external, 114, 115
  internal, 114, 115
  physical, 90
Courtesy, 50-52
Criticism, 7, 8
Criticism, fear of, 42, 61
Crying, 3, 4

Dating, 42, 52
Decision changing, 62
Decision-making, 58, 105, 106
Decision-making, scientific, 59-62
Decision ownership, 66, 67
Dependency, 116
Disappointment, 55
Disrespect, 53, 54
Driving, auto, 114
Drug abuse, 38

Emotional distancing, 109
Emotionality, excessive, 40, 41
Empathy, 18, 63
Environment
  emotional, 2, 3
  physical, 2, 70
Expectation
  age appropriate, 92
  positive, 88, 89
  unreasonable, 36, 37, 96

Failure
  fear of, 61
  temporary, 62, 89, 90
Fallibility, 36, 64, 124, 125
Fear
  appropriate, 5
  parental, 44
Feeling ventilation, 45
Firing, parental, 26
Forgiveness, 84
Freedom
  from speech, 17, 18
  of speech, 17, 18
  to fail, 74, 115, 116

Friends, selection of, 42, 43
Friendships, peer, 112

Game playing, 63
Gratitude, 36
Guest visitations, 94
Guilt, 29, 115, 116
Guilt by association, 64

Happiness, 122
Harris, Thomas A., 94
Help, professional, 125
Hubbard, Elbert, 123
Hypochondriac, 96

Identification, excessive, 119-21
Identity, 52, 53
Importance test, 87, 88
Incompetence, 77
Inconsistency, teen-age, 92, 93
Indecision, 61
Independence, 93, 94, 116, 117
Independence measure, 71-73, 118, 119
Information, decision-making, 59, 60
Information, vocational, 105, 106
Ingratitude modeling, 37
Interest tests, 103, 104
Intervention, parental, 80
Involvement, excessive, 117, 120, 121

Job, temporary, 104
Job satisfaction, 37
Judging, 74

Keller, Helen, 112, 113
Kidding, 25, 26, 52

Laziness, 91, 92
Learning
  complex, 6
  inappropriate, 3
  parental, 12, 13
Learning by association, 4
Limit enforcing, 88
Limit setting, 100
Listening, importance of, 18-20
Lying, 85, 86

Marijuana, 38, 39
Marital relationship, 119
Martyrs, parental, 119, 120
Meal preparation, 19, 20
Mealtime, 31, 32, 57
Mentor, 106
Message bombs, 22
Mistakes, fear of, 34

Models, peer, 42
Money, 116
Motive, unconscious, 82
Mussen, Paul H., 92

Natural consequences, 88
Need to be needed, 58, 109, 112
Negativism, parental 85-87
Nightengale, Earl, 77

Opinions
  children's, 65
  other's, 95
Overgeneralization, 64
Overinvolvement, parental, 97
Overloaded circuits, 97, 98
Overwatchfulness, 97

Peacemaker, 80
Peer influence, 58
Perfection, 124
Permission, 62-64
Permissiveness, 52, 53
Pleading behavior, 63, 66
Plutarch, 76
Power, arbitrary, 62
Predictability, parental, 98, 99
Prison, 39
Privacy, 51
Problem
  primary, 60
  secondary, 60
Problem formulation, 60
Property rights, 79-82
Prophecy, self fulfilling, 44, 49, 50, 64
Punishment, 76
Put-down statements, 50

Questions
  children's, 64, 65
  dysfunctional, 24, 25

Reinforcement, positive, 99
Relationships, peer, 79
Religion, 84-87
Requests, unreasonable, 95
Rescuing, parental, 115
Respect, 90
  definition of, 47
Responsibility
  age appropriate, 71-74
  avoidance, 82
  financial, 21, 116
  need for, 69

Ridicule, 42, 52
Risk
  physical, 13, 14
  vocational choice, 104
Role reversal, 65

School, 1, 17
School peers, 64
Security, 99, 112-14
Self-actualization, 34
Self-discipline, 105
Self-expectations, 98
Self-fulfilling prophecy, 44, 49, 50, 64
Self-image, 65, 67
Self-reliance, 82
Self-respect, 55
Self, responsibility for, 79
Self-trust, 43, 44
Sex change, psychological, 91
Sex education, 23, 24
Slonaker independence test, 71-73, 118, 119
Speech
  freedom from, 17
  freedom of, 48, 49
Standards, rigid, 86

Success, 33, 34, 89, 90
  assurance, 70
  excessive, 33, 34
Surprises, dysfunctional, 26

Task
  completion, 70
  complexity, 70-74
Television, 6
Temper tantrum, 45
Threats, 53
Time finding, 24
Trust, 43-45, 113
Truth, 49
Twain, Mark, 123

Unanimity, parental, 65, 66

Value system, 100
Values, 5, 6
Viewpoint differences, 95
Vocational choice, 104-7

Wages, children's, 75
Wilman, Erastus, 50
Why statements, 85, 86
Work, 69, 71-74, 76
Working mothers, 96

Teenagers Ahead